The Ultimate ENGAA Guide

UniAdmissions

ISBN 978-1-912557-05-9

2nd Edition

Published by *RAR Medical Services Limited*
www.uniadmissions.co.uk
info@uniadmissions.co.uk
Tel: 0208 068 0438

The Ultimate ENGAA Guide

250 Practice Questions

Madhivanan Elango
Dr Rohan Agarwal

UniAdmissions

About the Authors

Madhivanan graduated with a **1st class degree in Engineering** from the University of Cambridge coming in the top 10% of his year and specialising in bioengineering, instrumentation and control and mechanical engineering. In his final year, he completed a project on the automated diagnosis of otitis media and was awarded the 3rd Year Computer-based Project Prize.

He has won gold medals in the UK Mathematics and Chemistry Olympiads. Madhi has worked with UniAdmissions since 2016 and has successfully tutored many students into Oxbridge. In his spare time, Madhivanan enjoys badminton, chess and travelling.

Rohan is the **Director of Operations** at *UniAdmissions* and is responsible for its technical and commercial arms. He graduated from Gonville and Caius College, Cambridge and is a fully qualified doctor. Over the last five years, he has tutored hundreds of successful Oxbridge and Medical applicants. He has also authored ten books on admissions tests and interviews.

Rohan has taught physiology to undergraduates and interviewed medical school applicants for Cambridge. He has published research on bone physiology and writes education articles for the Independent and Huffington Post. In his spare time, Rohan enjoys playing the piano and table tennis.

PREFACE

The ENGAA (Engineering Admissions Assessment) is a relatively new test used by the University of Cambridge for undergraduate admissions considering recent changes to A Levels. There aren't many past papers for the exam so we hope the questions in this book will give you a realistic idea for what to expect on the day. We hope that you find this book useful for your ENGAA revision and welcome all feedback to improve future editions.

The test lasts 120 minutes split into two sections consisting wholly of multiple choice questions. All of the content is from your maths and physics curriculum at school so it really is a test of how you can apply the knowledge that you have in an unfamiliar context. The strict timings of the ENGAA also mean that you will have to think quickly- a skill that comes with practice.

While these tests do provide a wide range of questions reflecting what you will see on test day, please do not use this as your only resource. Remember that most of the knowledge for this test will come from the maths and physics that you are learning at school- this guide will hopefully highlight the important aspects that are relevant to the ENGAA.

Finally, remember that the ENGAA is a **challenging** and **time-pressured** exam that is designed to push you to your limits. It is different from school exams where high marks are to be expected so do not be disheartened when doing practice papers- everyone feels this way! Some of the questions will give you an idea of the types you will see at university- they are designed to make you think but also spark your interest. Think of the ENGAA as an opportunity to show the engineering admissions staff what you are really capable of!

Good luck!

Madhivanan Elango

The Basics

What is the ENGAA?

The Engineering Admissions Assessment (ENGAA) is a two-hour written exam taken by prospective Cambridge Engineering applicants.

What does the ENGAA consist of?

Section	Timing	SKILLS TESTED	Questions	Calculator
ONE	80 Minutes	1A: Maths and Physics 1B: Advanced Maths & Physics	28 MCQs 26 MCQs	Not Allowed
TWO	40 Minutes	Advanced Maths and Advanced Physics	17 MCQs	Not Allowed

Why is the ENGAA used?

Cambridge Engineering applicants tend to be a bright bunch and therefore usually have excellent grades with many having over 90% in all of their A level subjects. This means that competition is fierce – meaning that the universities must use the ENGAA to help differentiate between applicants.

When do I sit ENGAA?

The ENGAA takes place in the first week of November every year, normally on a Wednesday Morning.

Can I resit the ENGAA?

No, you can only sit the ENGAA once per admissions cycle.

Where do I sit the ENGAA?

You can usually sit the ENGAA at your school or college (ask your exams officer for more information). Alternatively, if your school isn't a registered test centre or you're not attending a school or college, you can sit the ENGAA at an authorised test centre.

Do I have to resit the ENGAA if I reapply?

Yes - you cannot use your score from any previous attempts.

How is the ENGAA Scored?

In section 1, each question carries one mark and there is no negative marking. In section 2, marks for each question are indicated alongside it. Unless stated otherwise, you will only score marks for correct answers if you show your working.

How is the ENGAA used?

Different Cambridge colleges will place different weightings on different components so it's important you find out as much information about how your marks will be used by emailing the college admissions office.

In general, the university will interview a high proportion of realistic applicants so the ENGAA score isn't vital for making the interview shortlist. However, it can play a huge role in the final decision after your interview.

General Advice

Start Early

It is much easier to prepare if you practice little and often. Start your preparation well in advance; ideally by mid September but at the latest by early October. This way you will have plenty of time to complete as many papers as you wish to feel comfortable and won't have to panic and cram just before the test, which is a much less effective and more stressful way to learn. In general, an early start will give you the opportunity to identify the complex issues and work at your own pace.

Prioritise

Some questions in the ENGAA can be long and complex – and given the intense time pressure you need to know your limits. It is essential that you don't get stuck with very difficult questions. If a question looks particularly long or complex, mark it for review and move on. You don't want to be caught 5 questions short at the end just because you took more than 3 minutes in answering a challenging multi-step physics question. If a question is taking too long, choose a sensible answer and move on. Remember that each question carries equal weighting and therefore, you should adjust your timing in accordingly. With practice and discipline, you can get very good at this and learn to maximise your efficiency.

Positive Marking

There are no penalties for incorrect answers in the ENGAA; you will gain one for each right answer and will not get one for each wrong or unanswered one. This provides you with the luxury that you can always guess should you absolutely be not able to figure out the right answer for a question or run behind time. Since each question provides you with 4 to 6 possible answers, you have a 16-25% chance of guessing correctly. Therefore, if you aren't sure (and are running short of time), then make an educated guess and move on.

Before 'guessing' you should try to eliminate a couple of answers to increase your chances of getting the question correct. For example, if a question has 5 options and you manage to eliminate 2 options- your chances of getting the question increase from 20% to 33%!

Avoid losing easy marks on other questions because of poor exam technique. Similarly, if you have failed to finish the exam, take the last 10 seconds to guess the remaining questions to at least give yourself a chance of getting them right.

Practice

This is the best way of familiarising yourself with the style of questions and the timing for this section. You are unlikely to be familiar with the style of questions when you first encounter them. Therefore, you want to be comfortable at using this before you sit the test.

Practising questions will put you at ease and make you more comfortable with the exam. The more comfortable you are, the less you will panic on the test day and the more likely you are to score highly. Initially, work through the questions at your own pace, and spend time carefully reading the questions and looking at any additional data. When it becomes closer to the test, **make sure you practice the questions under exam conditions**.

Past Papers

The ENGAA is a very new exam so there aren't many past papers available. Specimen papers are freely available online at **www.uniadmissions.co.uk/ENGAA**. Once you've worked your way through the questions in this book, you are highly advised to attempt them.

Repeat Questions

When checking through answers, pay particular attention to questions you have got wrong. If there is a worked answer, look through that carefully until you feel confident that you understand the reasoning, and then repeat the question without help to check that you can do it. If only the answer is given, have another look at the question and try to work out why that answer is correct. This is the best way to learn from your mistakes, and means you are less likely to make similar mistakes when it comes to the test.

The same applies for questions which you were unsure of and made an educated guess which was correct, even if you got it right. When working through this book, **make sure you highlight any questions you are unsure of**, this means you know to spend more time looking over them once marked.

Calculators

You are not permitted to use calculators two – thus, it is essential that you have strong numerical skills. For instance, you should be able to rapidly convert between percentages, decimals and fractions. You will seldom get questions that would require calculators but you would be expected to be able to arrive at a sensible estimate. Consider for example:

Estimate 3.962 x 2.322:

3.962 is approximately 4 and 2.323 is approximately 2.33 = 7/3.

Thus, $3.962 \times 2.322 \approx 4 \times \frac{7}{3} = \frac{28}{3} = 9.33$

Since you will rarely be asked to perform difficult calculations, you can use this as a signpost of if you are tackling a question correctly. For example, when solving a physics question in section 1, you end up having to divide 8,079 by 357- this should raise alarm bells as calculations in the ENGAA are rarely this difficult.

A word on timing...

"If you had all day to do your ENGAA, you would get 100%. But you don't."

Whilst this isn't completely true, it illustrates a very important point. Once you've practiced and know how to answer the questions, the clock is your biggest enemy. This seemingly obvious statement has one very important consequence. **The way to improve your ENGAA score is to improve your speed.** There is no magic bullet. But there are a great number of techniques that, with practice, will give you significant time gains, allowing you to answer more questions and score more marks.

Timing is tight throughout the ENGAA – **mastering timing is the first key to success**. Some candidates choose to work as quickly as possible to save up time at the end to check back, but this is generally not the best way to do it. ENGAA questions can have a lot of information in them – each time you start answering a question it takes time to get familiar with the instructions and information. By splitting the question into two sessions (the first run-through and the return-to-check) you double the amount of time you spend on familiarising yourself with the data, as you have to do it twice instead of only once. This costs valuable time.

In addition, candidates who do check back may spend 2–3 minutes doing so and yet not make any actual changes. Whilst this can be reassuring, it is a false reassurance as it is unlikely to have a significant effect on your actual score. Therefore it is usually best to pace yourself very steadily, aiming to spend the same amount of time on each question and finish the final question in a section just as time runs out. This reduces the time spent on re-familiarising with questions and maximises the time spent on the first attempt, gaining more marks.

It is essential that you don't get stuck with the hardest questions – no doubt there will be some. In the time spent answering only one of these you may miss out on answering three easier questions. If a question is taking too long, choose a sensible answer and move on. Never see this as giving up or in any way failing, rather it is the smart way to approach a test with a tight time limit.

With practice and discipline, you can get very good at this and learn to maximise your efficiency. It is not about being a hero and aiming for full marks – this is almost impossible and very much unnecessary (even for Cambridge!). It is about maximising your efficiency and gaining the maximum possible number of marks within the time you have.

> ***Top tip!*** Ensure that you take a watch that can show you the time in seconds into the exam. This will allow you have a much more accurate idea of the time you're spending on a question. In general, if you've spent >120 seconds on a section one question - move on regardless of how close you think you are to solving it.

Use the Options:

Some questions may try to overload you with information. When presented with large tables and data, it's essential you look at the answer options so you can focus your mind. This can allow you to reach the correct answer a lot more quickly. Consider the example below:

The table below shows the results of a study investigating antibiotic resistance in staphylococcus populations. A single staphylococcus bacterium is chosen at random from a similar population. Resistance to any one antibiotic is independent of resistance to others.

Antibiotic	Number of Bacteria tested	Number of Resistant Bacteria
Benzyl-penicillin	10^{11}	98
Chloramphenicol	10^{9}	1200
Metronidazole	10^{8}	256
Erythromycin	10^{5}	2

Calculate the probability that the bacterium selected will be resistant to all four drugs.

A 1 in 10^{6}
B 1 in 10^{12}
C 1 in 10^{20}
D 1 in 10^{25}
E 1 in 10^{30}
F 1 in 10^{35}

Looking at the options first makes it obvious that there is **no need to calculate exact values**- only in powers of 10. This makes your life a lot easier. If you hadn't noticed this, you might have spent well over 90 seconds trying to calculate the exact value when it wasn't even being asked for.

In other cases, you may actually be able to use the options to arrive at the solution quicker than if you had tried to solve the question as you normally would. Consider the example below:

A region is defined by the two inequalities: $x - y^2 > 1$ *and* $xy > 1$. Which of the following points is in the defined region?

A. (10,3)
B. (10,2)
C. (-10,3)
D. (-10,2)
E. (-10,-3)

Whilst it's possible to solve this question both algebraically or graphically by manipulating the identities, by far **the quickest way is to actually use the options**. Note that options C, D and E violate the second inequality, narrowing down to answer to either A or B. For A: $10 - 3^2 = 1$ and thus this point is on the boundary of the defined region and not actually in the region. Thus the answer is B (as $10-4 = 6 > 1$.)

In general, it pays dividends to look at the options briefly and see if they can help you arrive at the question more quickly. Get into this habit early – it may feel unnatural at first but it's guaranteed to save you time in the long run.

Keywords

If you're stuck on a question; pay particular attention to the options that contain key modifiers like "**always**", "**only**", "**all**" as examiners like using them to test if there are any gaps in your knowledge. E.g. the statement "arteries carry oxygenated blood" would normally be true; "All arteries carry oxygenated blood" would be false because the pulmonary artery carries deoxygenated blood.

SECTION 1

Section 1 tests Maths & Physics aptitude. The questions are split approximately evenly between GCSE level and A level. You have to answer 54 questions 80 minutes making this is a very time pressured section.

The questions can be quite difficult and it's easy to get bogged down. The intense time pressure of having to do one question every 90 seconds makes this a difficult section.

Gaps in Knowledge

In addition to GCSE level physics and maths, you are also expected to have a firm command of A-level topics. This can be a problem if you haven't studied these topics at school yet. A summary of the specification is provided later in the book but you are highly advised to go through the official ENGAA Specification and ensure that you have covered all examinable topics. An electronic copy of this can be obtained from **www.uniadmissions.co.uk/ENGAA**.

The questions in this book will help highlight any particular areas of weakness or gaps in your knowledge that you may have. Upon discovering these, make sure you take some time to revise these topics before carrying on – there is little to be gained by attempting questions with huge gaps in your knowledge.

Maths

Being confident with maths is extremely important for the ENGAA. Many students find that improving their numerical and algebraic skills usually results in big improvements in their section 1 and 2 scores. Maths pervades the ENGAA so if you find yourself consistently running out of time in practice papers, spending a few hours on brushing up your basic maths skills may do wonders for you.

SECTION 1: Physics

Physics Syllabus

- Calculate, manipulate and resolve Vectors and their components & resultants
- Calculate the moment of a force
- Difference between normal and frictional components of contact forces
- Concept of 'Limiting Equilibrium'
- Understand how to use the coefficient of Friction including $F = \mu R$ and $F \leq \mu R$
- Use of the equations of Motion
- Graphical interpretations of vectors + scalars
- Derivation + Integration of physical values e.g. Velocity from an acceleration-time graph
- Principle of conservation of momentum (including coalescence)+ Linear Momentum
- Principle of conservation of energy and its application to kinetic/gravitational potential energy
- Application of Newton's laws e.g.
    - Linear Motion of point masses
    - Modelling of objects moving vertically or on a planet
    - Objects connected by a rod or pulleys

Top tip! Knowing SI units is extremely useful because they allow you to **'work out' equations** if you ever forget them e.g. The units for density are kg/m^3. Since Kg is the SI unit for mass, and m^3 is represented by volume –the equation for density must be = Mass/Volume.

This can also work the other way, for example we know that the unit for Pressure is Pascal (Pa). But based on the fact that Pressure = Force/Area, a Pascal must be equivalent to N/m^2.

Multi-Step Questions

Most ENGAA physics questions require two step calculations. Consider the example:

A metal ball is released from the roof a 20 metre building. Assuming air resistance equals is negligible; calculate the velocity at which the ball hits the ground. [$g = 10ms^{-2}$]

A. 5 ms^{-1}
B. 10 ms^{-1}
C. 15 ms^{-1}
D. 20 ms^{-1}
E. 25 ms^{-1}

When the ball hits the ground, all of its gravitational potential energy has been converted to kinetic energy. Thus, $E_p = E_k$:

$$mg\Delta h = \frac{mv^2}{2}$$

Thus, $v = \sqrt{2gh} = \sqrt{2 \text{ x } 10 \text{ x } 20}$

$$= \sqrt{400} = 20ms^{-1}$$

Here, you were required to not only recall two equations but apply and rearrange them very quickly to get the answer; all in under 60 seconds. Thus, it is easy to understand why the physics questions are generally much harder than the biology and chemistry ones.

Note that if you were comfortable with basic Newtonian mechanics, you could have also solved this using a single suvat equation: $v^2 = u^2 + 2as$

$$v = \sqrt{2 \text{ x } 10 \text{ x } 20} = 20ms^{-1}$$

SI Units

Remember that in order to get the correct answer you must always work in SI units i.e. do your calculations in terms of metres (not centimetres) and kilograms (not grams), etc.

Formulas you MUST know:

Equations of Motion:

- $s = ut + 0.5at^2$
- $v = u + at$
- $a = (v-u)/t$
- $v^2 = u^2 + 2as$

Equations Relating to Force:

- Force = mass x acceleration
- Force = Momentum/Time
- Pressure = Force / Area
- Moment of a Force = Force x Distance
- Work done = Force x Displacement

Mechanics & Motion:

- Conservation of momentum $\Delta mv = 0$
- Force $F = \frac{\Delta mv}{t}$
- Angular velocity $\omega = \frac{v}{r} = 2\pi f$

Gravitational Forces

- Potential $V = \frac{Gm}{r}$
- Acceleration $a = \frac{GM}{r^2} = \frac{\partial V}{\partial r}$

Simple harmonic motion & oscillations

- Displacement $x = ACos(2\pi ft)$
- Acceleration $a = -(2\pi f)^2 x = -(2\pi f)^2\, ACos(2\pi ft)$
- Speed $v = \pm 2\pi f\sqrt{A^2 - x^2}$

Equations relating to Energy:

- Kinetic Energy = 0.5 mv^2
- Δ in Gravitational Potential Energy = $mg\Delta h$
- Energy Efficiency = (Useful energy/ Total energy) x 100%

Equations relating to Power:

- Power = Work done / time
- Power = Energy transferred / time
- Power = Force x velocity

For objects in equilibrium:

- Sum of Clockwise moments = Sum of Anti-clockwise moments
- Sum of all resultant forces = 0

Electrical Equations:

- $Q = It$
- $V = IR$
- $P = IV = I^2R = V^2/R$
- e.m.f $\varepsilon = \frac{E}{Q} = I(R + r)$
- Resistivity $\rho = \frac{RA}{l}$
- Resistors in series $R = \sum_{i=1}^{n} R_i$
- Resistors in parallel s $R = \sum_{i=1}^{n} \frac{1}{R_i}$

Magnetic Fields:

- Magnetic flux $\emptyset = BA$
- Magnetic flux linkage $\emptyset N = BAN$
- Magnitude of induced e.m.f $\varepsilon = N\frac{\Delta\emptyset}{\Delta t}$

For Transformers: $\frac{V_p}{V_s} = \frac{n_p}{n_s}$ where:

- V: Potential difference
- *n*: Number of turns
- *p*: Primary
- *s*: Secondary

Waves

- Speed $c = f\,\lambda$
- Period $T = \frac{1}{f}$
- Snell's law $n_1 sin\theta_1 = n_2 sin\theta_2$

Radioactivity

- Decay $N = N_0 e^{-\lambda t}$
- Half life $T_{1/2} = \frac{ln2}{\lambda}$
- Activity $A = \lambda N$
- Energy $E = mc^2$

Other:

- Weight = mass x g
- Density = Mass / Volume
- Momentum = Mass x Velocity
- g = 9.81 ms^{-2} (unless otherwise stated)

Factor	Text	Symbol
10^{12}	Tera	T
10^{9}	Giga	G
10^{6}	Mega	M
10^{3}	Kilo	k
10^{2}	Hecto	h
10^{-1}	Deci	d
10^{-2}	Centi	c
10^{-3}	Milli	m
10^{-6}	Micro	µ
10^{-9}	Nano	n
10^{-12}	Pico	p

Physics Questions

Question 1:
Which of the following statements are **FALSE**?

A. Electromagnetic waves cause things to heat up.
B. X-rays and gamma rays can knock electrons out of their orbits.
C. Loud sounds can make objects vibrate.
D. Wave power can be used to generate electricity.
E. Since waves carry energy away, the source of a wave loses energy.
F. The amplitude of a wave determines its mass.

Question 2:
A spacecraft is analysing a newly discovered exoplanet. A rock of unknown mass falls on the planet from a height of 30 m. Given that $g = 5.4\ ms^{-2}$ on the planet, calculate the speed of the rock when it hits the ground and the time it took to fall.

	Speed (ms^{-1})	Time (s)
A	18	3.3
B	18	3.1
C	12	3.3
D	10	3.7
E	9	2.3
F	1	0.3

Question 3:
A canoe floating on the sea rises and falls 7 times in 49 seconds. The waves pass it at a speed of 5 ms^{-1}. How long are the waves?

A. 12 m
B. 22 m
C. 25 m
D. 35 m
E. 57 m
F. 75 m

Question 4:

Miss Orrell lifts her 37.5 kg bike for a distance of 1.3 m in 5 s. The acceleration of free fall is 10 ms^{-2}. What is the average power that she develops?

A. 9.8 W
B. 12.9 W
C. 57.9 W
D. 79.5 W
E. 97.5W
F. 98.0 W

Question 5:
A truck accelerates at 5.6 ms^{-2} from rest for 8 seconds. Calculate the final speed and the distance travelled in 8 seconds.

	Final Speed (ms^{-1})	Distance (m)
A	40.8	119.2
B	40.8	129.6
C	42.8	179.2
D	44.1	139.2
E	44.1	179.7
F	44.2	129.2
G	44.8	179.2
H	44.8	179.7

Question 6:

Which of the following statements is true when a sky diver jumps out of a plane?

A. The sky diver leaves the plane and will accelerate until the air resistance is greater than their weight.
B. The sky diver leaves the plane and will accelerate until the air resistance is less than their weight.
C. The sky diver leaves the plane and will accelerate until the air resistance equals their weight.
D. The sky diver leaves the plane and will accelerate until the air resistance equals their weight squared.
E. The sky diver will travel at a constant velocity after leaving the plane.

Question 7:

A 100 g apple falls on Isaac's head from a height of 20 m. Calculate the apple's momentum before the point of impact. Take $g = 10\ ms^{-2}$

A. 0.1 $kgms^{-1}$	C. 1 $kgms^{-1}$	E. 10 $kgms^{-1}$
B. 0.2 $kgms^{-1}$	D. 2 $kgms^{-1}$	F. 20 $kgms^{-1}$

Question 8:

Which of the following do all electromagnetic waves all have in common?

1. They can travel through a vacuum.
2. They can be reflected.
3. They are the same length.
4. They have the same amount of energy.
5. They can be polarised.

A. 1, 2 and 3 only	D. 3 and 4 only
B. 1, 2, 3 and 4 only	E. 1, 2 and 5 only
C. 4 and 5 only	F. 1 and 5 only

Question 9:

A battery with an internal resistance of 0.8 Ω and e.m.f of 36 V is used to power a drill with resistance 1 Ω. What is the current in the circuit when the drill is connected to the power supply?

A. 5 A
B. 10 A
C. 15 A
D. 20 A
E. 25 A
F. 30 A

✱ **Question 10:**

Officer Bailey throws a 20 g dart at a speed of 100 ms^{-1}. It strikes the dartboard and is brought to rest in 10 milliseconds. Calculate the average force exerted on the dart by the dartboard.

A. 0.2 N
B. 2 N
C. 20 N
D. 200 N
E. 2,000 N
F. 20,000 N

Question 11:

Professor Huang lifts a 50 kg bag through a distance of 0.7 m in 3 s. What average power does she develop to 3 significant figures? Take $g = 10ms^{-2}$

A. 112 W
B. 113 W
C. 114 W
D. 115 W
E. 116 W
F. 117 W

✱ **Question 12:**

An electric scooter is travelling at a speed of 30 ms^{-1} and is kept going against a 50 N frictional force by a driving force of 300 N in the direction of motion. Given that the engine runs at 200 V, calculate the current in the scooter.

A. 4.5 A
B. 45 A
C. 450 A
D. 4,500 A
E. 45,000 A
F. More information needed.

Question 13:

Which of the following statements about the physical definition of work are correct?

1. $Work\ done = \frac{Force}{distance}$
2. The unit of work is equivalent to $Kgms^{-2}$.
3. Work is defined as a force causing displacement of the body upon which it acts.

A. Only 1
B. Only 2
C. Only 3
D. 1 and 2
E. 2 and 3
F. 1 and 3

✱ **Question 14:**

Which of the following statements about kinetic energy are correct?

1. It is defined as $E_k = \frac{mv^2}{2}$
2. The unit of kinetic energy is equivalent to Pa x m^3.
3. Kinetic energy is equal to the amount of energy needed to decelerate the body in question from its current speed.

A. Only 1
B. Only 2
C. Only 3
D. 1 and 2
E. 2 and 3
F. 1 and 3
→ G. 1, 2 and 3

✱ **Question 15:**

In relation to radiation, which of the following statements is **FALSE**?

A. Radiation is the emission of energy in the form of waves or particles.
B. Radiation can be either ionizing or non-ionizing.
C. Gamma radiation has very high energy.
→ D. Alpha radiation is of higher energy than beta radiation.
E. X-rays are an example of wave radiation.

Question 16:

In relation to the physical definition of half-life, which of the following statements are correct?

1. In radioactive decay, the half-life is independent of atom type and isotope.
2. Half-life is defined as the time required for exactly half of the entities to decay.
3. Half-life applies to situations of both exponential and non-exponential decay.

A. Only 1
B. Only 2
C. Only 3
D. 1 and 2
E. 2 and 3
F. 1 and 3

Question 17:

In relation to nuclear fusion, which of the following statements is **FALSE**?

A. Nuclear fusion is initiated by the absorption of neutrons.
B. Nuclear fusion describes the fusion of hydrogen atoms to form helium atoms.
C. Nuclear fusion releases great amounts of energy.
D. Nuclear fusion requires high activation temperatures.
E. All of the statements above are false.

Question 18:

In relation to nuclear fission, which of the following statements is correct?

A. Nuclear fission is the basis of many nuclear weapons.
B. Nuclear fission is triggered by the shooting of neutrons at unstable atoms.
C. Nuclear fission can trigger chain reactions.
D. Nuclear fission commonly results in the emission of ionizing radiation.
E. All of the above.

Question 19:

Two identical resistors (R_a and R_b) are connected in a series circuit. Which of the following statements are true?

1. The current through both resistors is the same.
2. The voltage through both resistors is the same.
3. The voltage across the two resistors is given by Ohm's Law.

A. Only 1
B. Only 2
C. Only 3
D. 1 and 2
E. 2 and 3
F. 1 and 3
G. 1, 2 and 3
H. None of the statements are true.

Question 20:

The Sun is 8 light-minutes away from the Earth. Estimate the circumference of the Earth's orbit around the Sun. Assume that the Earth is in a circular orbit around the Sun. Speed of light = 3×10^8 ms^{-1}

A. 10^{24} m
B. 10^{21} m
C. 10^{18} m
D. 10^{15} m
E. 10^{12} m
F. 10^{9} m

Question 21:

Which of the following statements are true?

1. Speed is the same as velocity.
2. The internationally standardised unit for speed is ms^{-2}.
3. Velocity = distance/time.

A. Only 1
B. Only 2
C. Only 3
D. 1 and 2
E. 2 and 3
F. 1 and 3
G. 1, 2 and 3
H. None of the statements are true.

Question 22:

Which of the following statements best defines Ohm's Law?

A. The current through an insulator between two points is indirectly proportional to the potential difference across the two points.
B. The current through an insulator between two points is directly proportional to the potential difference across the two points.
C. The current through a conductor between two points is inversely proportional to the potential difference across the two points.
D. The current through a conductor between two points is proportional to the square of the potential difference across the two points.
E. The current through a conductor between two points is directly proportional to the potential difference across the two points.

Question 23:

Which of the following statements regarding Newton's Second Law are correct?

1. For objects at rest, Resultant Force must be 0 Newtons
2. Force = Mass x Acceleration
3. Force = Rate of change of Momentum

A. Only 1
B. Only 2
C. Only 3
D. 1 and 2
E. 2 and 3
F. 1 and 3
G. 1, 2 and 3

Question 24:

Which of the following equations concerning electrical circuits are correct?

1. $Charge = \frac{Voltage\ x\ time}{Resistance}$
2. $Charge = \frac{Power\ x\ time}{Voltage}$
3. $Charge = \frac{Current\ \ x\ time}{Resistance}$

A. Only 1
B. Only 2
C. Only 3
D. 1 and 2
E. 2 and 3
F. 1 and 3
G. 1, 2 and 3
H. None of the equations are correct.

Question 25:

An elevator has a mass of 1,600 kg and is carrying passengers that have a combined mass of 200 kg. A constant frictional force of 4,000 N retards its motion upward. What force must the motor provide for the elevator to move with an upward acceleration of 1 ms^{-2}? Assume: $g = 10\ ms^{-2}$

A. 1,190 N
B. 11,900 N
C. 18,000 N
D. 22,000 N
E. 23,800 N

Question 26:

A 1,000 kg car accelerates from rest at 5 ms^{-2} for 10 s. Then, a braking force is applied to bring it to rest within 20 seconds. What distance has the car travelled?

A. 125 m
B. 250 m
C. 650 m
D. 750 m
E. 1,200 m
F. More information needed

✱ **Question 27:**

An electric heater is connected to 120 V mains by a copper wire that has a resistance of 8 ohms. What is the power of the heater?

A. 90 W
B. 180 W
C. 900 W
D. 1800 W
E. 9,000W
F. 18,000 W
→ G. More information needed.

internal resistance

Question 28:

In a particle accelerator electrons are accelerated through a potential difference of 40 MV and emerge with an energy of 40MeV (1 MeV = 1.60 x 10^{-13} J). Each pulse contains 5,000 electrons. The current is zero between pulses. Assuming that the electrons have zero energy prior to being accelerated what is the power delivered by the electron beam?

A. 1 kW
B. 10 kW
C. 100 kW
D. 1,000 kW
E. 10,000 kW
F. More information needed

✱ **Question 29:**

Which of the following statements is true?

A. When an object is in equilibrium with its surroundings, there is no energy transferred to or from the object and so its temperature remains constant.
→ B. When an object is in equilibrium with its surroundings, it radiates and absorbs energy at the same rate and so its temperature remains constant.
C. Radiation is faster than convection but slower than conduction.
D. Radiation is faster than conduction but slower than convection.
E. None of the above.

Question 30:

A 6kg block is pulled from rest along a horizontal frictionless surface by a constant horizontal force of 12 N. Calculate the speed of the block after it has moved 300 cm.

A. $2\sqrt{3}\, ms^{-1}$

B. $4\sqrt{3}\, ms^{-1}$

C. $4\sqrt{3}\, ms^{-1}$

D. $12\, ms^{-1}$

E. $\sqrt{\frac{3}{2}}\, ms^{-1}$

Question 31:

A 100 V heater heats 1.5 litres of pure water from 10°C to 50°C in 50 minutes. Given that 1 kg of pure water requires 4,000 J to raise its temperature by 1°C, calculate the resistance of the heater.

A. 12.5 ohms

B. 25 ohms

C. 125 ohms

D. 250 ohms

E. 500 ohms

F. 850 ohms

Question 32:

Which of the following statements are true?

1. Nuclear fission is the basis of nuclear energy.
2. Following fission, the resulting atoms are a different element to the original one.
3. Nuclear fission often results in the production of free neutrons and photons.

A. Only 1

B. Only 2

C. Only 3

D. 1 and 2

E. 2 and 3

F. 1 and 3

G. 1, 2 and 3

H. None of the statements are true

Question 33:

Which of the following statements are true? Assume $g = 10\ ms^{-2}$.

1. Gravitational potential energy is defined as $\Delta E_p = m \times g \times \Delta h$.
2. Gravitational potential energy is a measure of the work done against gravity.
3. A reservoir situated 1 km above ground level with 10^6 litres of water has a potential energy of 1 Giga Joule.

A. Only 1
B. Only 2
C. Only 3
D. 1 and 2
E. 2 and 3
F. 1 and 3
G. 1, 2 and 3
H. None of the statements are true

Question 34:

Which of the following statements are correct in relation to Newton's 3rd law?

1. For every action there is an equal and opposite reaction.
2. According to Newton's 3rd law, there are no isolated forces.
3. Rockets cannot accelerate in deep space because there is nothing to generate an equal and opposite force.

A. Only 1
B. Only 2
C. Only 3
D. 1 and 2
E. 2 and 3
F. 1 and 3

Question 35:

Which of the following statements are correct?

1. Positively charged objects have gained electrons.
2. Electrical charge in a circuit over a period of time can be calculated if the voltage and resistance are known.
3. Objects can be charged by friction.

A. Only 1
B. Only 2
C. Only 3
D. 1 and 2
E. 2 and 3
F. 1 and 3
G. 1, 2 and 3

Question 36:

Which of the following statements is true?

A. The gravitational force between two objects is independent of their mass.
B. Each planet in the solar system exerts a gravitational force on the Earth.
C. For satellites in a geostationary orbit, acceleration due to gravity is equal and opposite to the lift from engines.
D. Two objects that are dropped from the Eiffel tower will always land on the ground at the same time if they have the same mass.
E. All of the above.
F. None of the above.

Question 37:
Which of the following best defines an electrical conductor?

A. Conductors are usually made from metals and they conduct electrical charge in multiple directions.
B. Conductors are usually made from non-metals and they conduct electrical charge in multiple directions.
C. Conductors are usually made from metals and they conduct electrical charge in one fixed direction.
D. Conductors are usually made from non-metals and they conduct electrical charge in one fixed direction.
E. Conductors allow the passage of electrical charge with zero resistance because they contain freely mobile charged particles.
F. Conductors allow the passage of electrical charge with maximal resistance because they contain charged particles that are fixed and static.

Question 38:
An 800 kg compact car delivers 20% of its power output to its wheels. If the car has a mileage of 30 miles/gallon and travels at a speed of 60 miles/hour, how much power is delivered to the wheels? 1 gallon of petrol contains 9×10^{8} J.

A. 10 kW
B. 20 kW
C. 40 kW
D. 50 kW
E. 100 kW

Question 39:
Which of the following statements about beta radiation are true?

1. After a beta particle is emitted, the atomic mass number is unchanged.
2. Beta radiation can penetrate paper but not aluminium foil.
3. A beta particle is emitted from the nucleus of the atom when an electron changes into a neutron.

A. 1 only
B. 2 only
C. 1 and 3
D. 1 and 2
E. 2 and 3
F. 1, 2 and 3

Question 40:

A car with a weight of 15,000 N is travelling at a speed of 15 ms^{-1} when it crashes into a wall and is brought to rest in 10 milliseconds. Calculate the average braking force exerted on the car by the wall. Take $g = 10\ ms^{-2}$

A. $1.25 \times 10^4 N$
B. $1.25 \times 10^5 N$
C. $1.25 \times 10^6 N$
D. $2.25 \times 10^4 N$
E. $2.25 \times 10^5 N$
F. $2.25 \times 10^6 N$

Question 41:
Which of the following statements are correct?

1. Electrical insulators are usually metals e.g. copper.
2. The flow of charge through electrical insulators is extremely low.
3. Electrical insulators can be charged by rubbing them together.

A. Only 1
B. Only 2
C. Only 3
D. 1 and 2
E. 2 and 3
F. 1 and 3
G. 1, 2 and 3

The following information is needed for Questions 42 and 43:

The graph below represents a car's movement. At t=0 the car's displacement was 0 m.

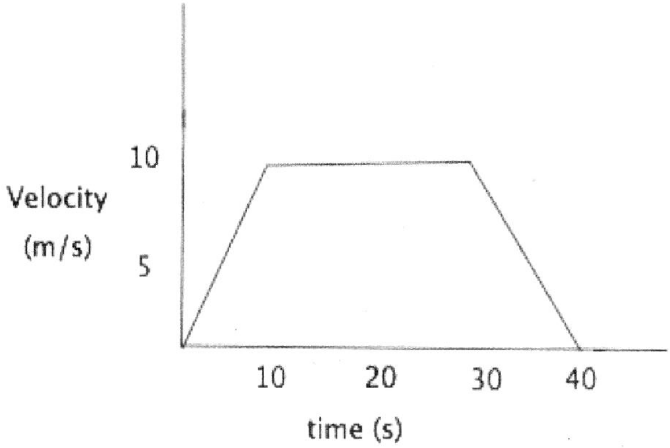

Question 42:
Which of the following statements are **NOT true**?

1. The car is reversing after t = 30.
2. The car moves with constant acceleration from t = 0 to t = 10.
3. The car moves with constant speed from t = 10 to t = 30.

A. 1 only
B. 2 only
C. 3 only
D. 1 and 3
E. 1 and 2
F. 2 and 3
G. 1, 2 and 3

Question 43:
Calculate the distance travelled by the car.

A. 200 m
B. 300 m
C. 350 m
D. 400 m
E. 500 m
F. More information needed

Question 44:

A 1,000 kg rocket is launched during a thunderstorm and reaches a constant velocity 30 seconds after launch. Suddenly, a strong gust of wind acts on it for 5 seconds with a force of 10,000 N in the direction of movement.
What is the resulting change in velocity?

A. 0.5 ms^{-1}
B. 5 ms^{-1}
C. 50 ms^{-1}
D. 500 ms^{-1}
E. 5000 ms^{-1}
F. More information needed

Question 45:
A 0.5 tonne crane lifts a 0.01 tonne wardrobe by 100 cm in 5,000 milliseconds.
Calculate the average power developed by the crane. Take $g = 10\ ms^{-2}$.

A. 0.2 W
B. 2 W
C. 5 W
D. 20 W
E. 50 W
F. More information needed

Question 46:
A 20 V battery is connected to a circuit consisting of a 1 Ω and 2 Ω resistor in parallel. Calculate the overall current of the circuit.

A. 6.67 A
B. 8 A
C. 10 A
D. 12 A
E. 20 A
F. 30 A

Question 47:
Which of the following statements is correct?

A. The speed of light changes when it enters water.
B. The speed of light changes when it leaves water.
C. The direction of light changes when it enters water.
D. The direction of light changes when it leaves water.
E. All of the above.
F. None of the above.

Question 48:
In a parallel circuit, a 60 V battery is connected to two branches. Branch A contains 6 identical 5 Ω resistors and branch B contains 2 identical 10 Ω resistors.

Calculate the current in branches A and B.

	I_A (A)	I_B (A)
A	0	6
B	6	0
C	2	3
D	3	2
E	3	3
F	1	5
G	5	1

Question 49:

Calculate the voltage of an electrical circuit that has a power output of 50,000,000,000 nW and a current of 0.000000004 GA.

A. 0.0125 GV
B. 0.0125 MV
C. 0.0125 kV
D. 0.0125 V
E. 0.0125 mV
F. 0.0125 μV
G. 0.0125 nV

Question 50:

Which of the following statements about radioactive decay is correct?

A. Radioactive decay is highly predictable.
B. An unstable element will continue to decay until it reaches a stable nuclear configuration.
C. All forms of radioactive decay release gamma rays.
D. All forms of radioactive decay release X-rays.
E. An atom's nuclear charge is unchanged after it undergoes alpha decay.
F. None of the above.

Question 51:

A circuit contains three identical resistors of unknown resistance connected in series with a 15 V battery. The power output of the circuit is 60 W. Calculate the overall resistance of the circuit when two further identical resistors are added to it.

A. 0.125 Ω
B. 1.25 Ω
C. 3.75 Ω
D. 6.25 Ω
E. 18.75 Ω
F. More information needed.

Question 52:

A 5,000 kg tractor's engine uses 1 litre of fuel to move 0.1 km. 1 ml of the fuel contains 20 kJ of energy.

Calculate the engine's efficiency. Take $g = 10\ ms^{-2}$

A. 2.5 %
B. 25 %
C. 38 %
D. 50 %
E. 75 %
F. More information needed.

Question 53:

Which of the following statements are correct?

1. Electromagnetic induction occurs when a wire moves relative to a magnet.
2. Electromagnetic induction occurs when a magnetic field changes.
3. An electrical current is generated when a coil rotates in a magnetic field.

A. Only 1
B. Only 2
C. Only 3
D. 1 and 2
E. 2 and 3
F. 1 and 3
G. 1, 2 and 3

Question 54:

Which of the following statements are correct regarding parallel circuits?

1. The current flowing through a branch is dependent on the branch's resistance.
2. The total current flowing into the branches is equal to the total current flowing out of the branches.
3. An ammeter will always give the same reading regardless of its location in the circuit.

A. Only 1
B. Only 2
C. Only 3
D. 1 and 2
E. 2 and 3
F. 1 and 3
G. All of the above

Question 55:

Which of the following statements regarding series circuits are true?

1. The overall resistance of a circuit is given by the sum of all resistors in the circuit.
2. Electrical current moves from the positive terminal to the negative terminal.
3. Electrons move from the positive terminal to the negative terminal.

A. Only 1
B. Only 2
C. Only 3
D. 1 and 2
E. 2 and 3
F. 1 and 3

Question 56:

The graphs below show current vs. voltage plots for 4 different electrical components.

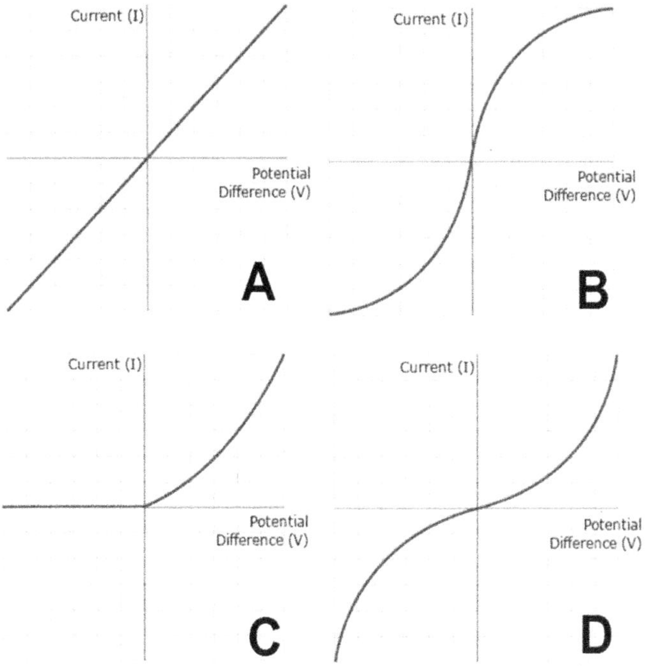

Which of the following graphs represents a resistor at constant temperature, and which a filament lamp?

	Fixed Resistor	Filament Lamp
A	A	B
B	A	C
C	A	D
D	C	A
E	C	C
F	C	D

Question 57:

Which of the following statements are true about vectors?

A. Vectors can be added or subtracted.
B. All vector quantities have a defined magnitude.
C. All vector quantities have a defined direction.
D. Displacement is an example of a vector quantity.
E. All of the above.
F. None of the above.

Question 58:

The acceleration due to gravity on the Earth is six times greater than that on the moon. Dr Tyson records the weight of a rock as 250 N on the moon.

Calculate the rock's density given that it has a volume of 250 cm^3. Take $g_{Earth} = 10\ ms^{-2}$

A. 0.2 kg/cm^3
B. 0.5 kg/cm^3
C. 0.6 kg/cm^3
D. 0.7 kg/cm^3
E. 0.8 kg/cm^3
F. More information needed.

Question 59:

A radioactive element X_{78}^{225} undergoes alpha decay. What is the atomic mass and atomic number after 5 alpha particles have been released?

	Mass Number	Atomic Number
A	200	56
B	200	58
C	205	64
D	205	68
E	215	58
F	215	73
G	225	78
H	225	83

Question 60:

A 20 A current passes through a circuit with resistance of 10 Ω. The circuit is connected to a transformer that contains a primary coil with 5 turns and a secondary coil with 10 turns. Calculate the potential difference exiting the transformer.

A. 100 V
B. 200 V
C. 400 V
D. 500 V
E. 2,000 V
F. 4,000 V
G. 5,000 V

Question 61:

A metal sphere of unknown mass is dropped from an altitude of 1 km and reaches terminal velocity 300 m before it hits the ground. Given that resistive forces do a total of 10 kJ of work for the last 100 m before the ball hits the ground, calculate the mass of the ball. Take $g = 10ms^{-2}$.

A. 1 kg
B. 2 kg
C. 5 kg
D. 10 kg
E. 20 kg
F. More information needed.

Question 62:

Which of the following statements is true about the electromagnetic spectrum?

A. The wavelength of ultraviolet waves is shorter than that of x-rays.
B. For waves in the electromagnetic spectrum, wavelength is directly proportional to frequency.
C. Most electromagnetic waves can be stopped with a thin layer of aluminium.
D. Waves in the electromagnetic spectrum travel at the speed of sound.
E. Humans are able to visualise the majority of the electromagnetic spectrum.
F. None of the above.

Question 63:

In relation to the Doppler Effect, which of the following statements are true?

1. If an object emitting a wave moves towards the sensor, the wavelength increases and frequency decreases.
2. An object that originally emitted a wave of a wavelength of 20 mm followed by a second reading delivering a wavelength of 15 mm is moving towards the sensor.
3. The faster the object is moving away from the sensor, the greater the increase in frequency.

A. Only 1
B. Only 2
C. Only 3
D. 1 and 2
E. 1 and 3
F. 2 and 3
G. 1, 2 and 3
H. None of the above statements are true.

Question 64:

A 5 g bullet is travels at 1 km/s and hits a brick wall. It penetrates 50 cm before being brought to rest 100 ms after impact. Calculate the average braking force exerted by the wall on the bullet.

A. 50 N
B. 500 N
C. 5,000 N
D. 50,000 N
E. 500,000 N
F. More information needed.

Question 65:

Polonium (Po) is a highly radioactive element that has no known stable isotope. Po^{210} undergoes radioactive decay to Pb^{206} and Y. Calculate the number of protons in 10 moles of *Y*. [Avogadro's Constant = 6×10^{23}]

A. 0
B. 1.2×10^{24}
C. 1.2×10^{25}
D. 2.4×10^{24}
E. 2.4×10^{25}
F. More information needed

Question 66:

Dr Sale measures the background radiation in a nuclear wasteland to be 1,000 Bq. He then detects a spike of 16,000 Bq from a nuclear rod made up of an unknown material. 300 days later, he visits and can no longer detect a reading higher than 1,000 Bq from the rod, even though it hasn't been disturbed.

What is the longest possible half-life of the nuclear rod?

A. 25 days
B. 50 days
C. 75 days
D. 100 days
E. 150 days
F. More information needed

Question 67:

A radioactive element Y_{89}^{200} undergoes a series of beta (β^-) and gamma decays. What are the number of protons and neutrons in the element after the emission of 5 beta particles and 2 gamma waves?

	Protons	Neutrons
A	79	101
B	84	111
C	84	116
D	89	111
E	89	106
F	94	111
G	94	106
H	109	111

Question 68:

Most symphony orchestras tune to 'standard pitch' (frequency = 440 Hz). When they are tuning, sound directly from the orchestra reaches audience members that are 500 m away in 1.5 seconds.

Estimate the wavelength of 'standard pitch'.

A. 0.05 m
B. 0.5 m
C. 0.75 m
D. 1.5 m
E. 15 m
F. More information needed

Question 69:

A 1 kg cylindrical artillery shell with a radius of 50 mm is fired at a speed of 200 ms^{-1}. It strikes an armour plated wall and is brought to rest in 500 μs.

Calculate the average pressure exerted on the entire shell by the wall at the time of impact.

A. 5×10^6 Pa
B. 5×10^7 Pa
C. 5×10^8 Pa
D. 5×10^9 Pa
E. 5×10^{10} Pa
F. More information needed

Question 70:

A 1,000 W display fountain launches 120 litres of water straight up every minute. Given that the fountain is 10% efficient, calculate the maximum possible height that the stream of water could reach.
Assume that there is negligible air resistance and $g = 10\ ms^{-2}$.

A. 1 m
B. 5 m
C. 10 m
D. 20 m
E. 50m
F. More information needed

Question 71

In relation to transformers, which of the following is true?

1. Step up transformers increase the voltage leaving the transformer.
2. In step down transformers, the number of turns in the primary coil is smaller than in the secondary coil.
3. For transformers that are 100% efficient: $I_p V_p = I_s V_s$

A. Only 1
B. Only 2
C. Only 3
D. 1 and 2
E. 1 and 3
F. 2 and 3
G. 1, 2 and 3
H. None of the above.

Question 72:

The half-life of Carbon-14 is 5,730 years. A bone is found that contains 6.25% of the amount of C^{14} that would be found in a modern one. How old is the bone?

A. 11,460 years
B. 17,190 years
C. 22,920 years
D. 28,650 years
E. 34,380 years
F. 40,110 years

Question 73:

A wave has a velocity of 2,000 mm/s and a wavelength of 250 cm. What is its frequency in MHz?

A. 8×10^{-3} MHz
B. 8×10^{-4} MHz
C. 8×10^{-5} MHz
D. 8×10^{-6} MHz
E. 8×10^{-7} MHz
F. 8×10^{-8} MHz

Question 74:

A radioactive element has a half-life of 25 days. After 350 days it has a count rate of 50. What was its original count rate?

A. 102,400
B. 162,240
C. 204,800
D. 409,600
E. 819,200
F. 1,638,400
G. 3,276,800

Question 75:

Which of the following units is **NOT** equivalent to a Volt (V)?

A. $A\Omega$
B. WA^{-1}
C. $Nms^{-1}A^{-1}$
D. NmC
E. JC^{-1}
F. $JA^{-1}s^{-1}$

Advanced Physics Questions

Question 76:

A ball is swung in a vertical circle from a string (of negligible mass). What is the minimum speed at the top of the arc for it to continue in a circular path?

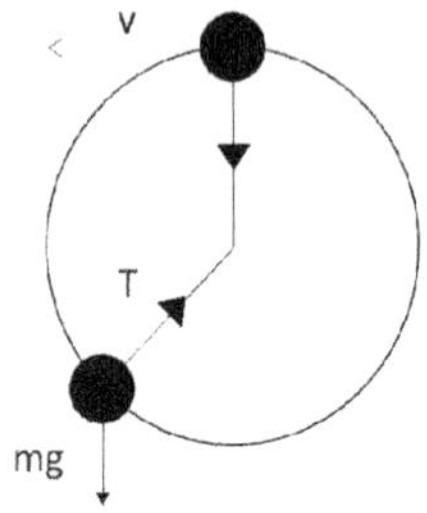

A. 0
B. mgr
C. $2r^2$
D. mg
E. $\sqrt{gr}$

Question 77:

A person pulls on a rope at 60° to the horizontal to exert a force on a mass m as shown. What is the power needed to move the mass up the 30° incline at a constant velocity, v, given a friction force F?

A. $\left(mg + \frac{F}{2}\right)v$
B. $\frac{mg}{\sqrt{2}} - F$
C. $\left(\frac{mg}{2}\right)v$
D. $\sqrt{2}Fv$
E. $\left(\frac{mg}{2} + F\right)v$

Question 78:

What is the maximum speed of a point mass, m, suspended from a string of length l, (a pendulum) if it is released from an angle θ where the string is taught?

A. $2gl(1-\cos(\theta))$

B. $2gl(1-\sin(\theta))$

C. $\sqrt{2gl(1-\cos(\theta))}$

D. $\sqrt{2gl(1-\sin(\theta))}$

E. $\sqrt{2gl(1-\cos^2(\theta))}$

Question 79:

Two spheres of equal mass, m, one at rest and one moving at velocity u1 towards the other as shown. After the collision, they move at angles φ and θ from the initial velocity u1 at respective velocities v_1 and v_2 where $v_2 = 2v_1$. What is the angle θ?

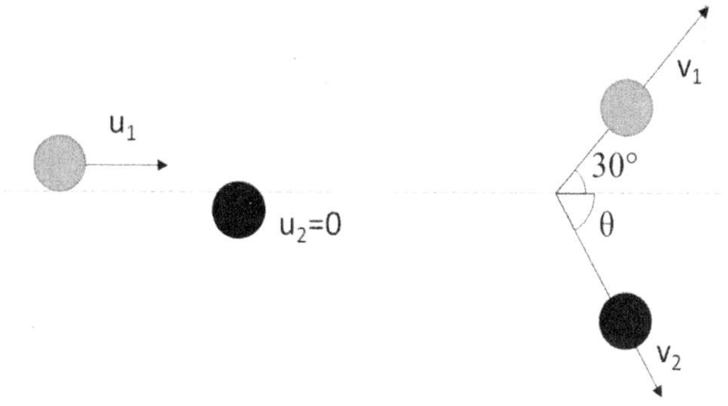

A. 0°

B. sin(50)

C. 30°

D. 45°

E. 90°

Question 80:

The first ball is three times the mass of the others. If this is an elastic collision, how many of the other ball move and at what velocity after the collision?

	Number of balls	Velocity
A	1	3v
B	1	v/3
C	3	v/3
D	3	v
E	3	$\sqrt{v}$

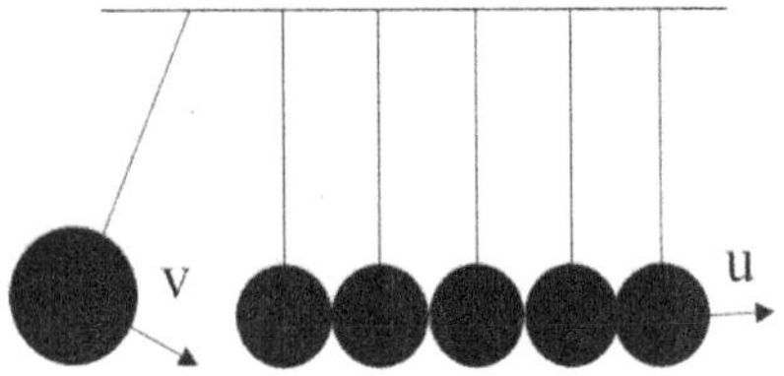

Question 81:

A ball is kicked over a 3 m fence from 6 m away with an initial height of zero. It does not strike the fence and lands 6m behind it. Assuming no air resistance, what is the minimum angle the ball must leave the ground at to make it over the fence?

A. $\arctan(1)$
B. $\arctan\left(\frac{1}{2}\right)$
C. $\arctan(2)$
D. 30°
E. $\arccos\left(\frac{-1}{2}\right)$

Question 82:

A mass on a spring of spring constant k is in simple harmonic motion at frequency f. If the mass is halved and the spring constant is double, by what factor will the frequency of oscillation change?

A. Stay the same
B. 2
C. 4
D. $\frac{1}{2}$
E. $\sqrt{2}$

Question 83:

A ball is dropped from 3 m above the ground and rebounds to a maximum height of 1 m. How much kinetic energy does it have just before hitting the ground and at the top of its bounce, and what is the maximum speed the ball reaches in any direction?

	E_k at Bottom	E_k at Top	Max Speed
A	0	30m	$2\sqrt{15}$
B	0	30m	30
C	30m	0	$2\sqrt{15}$
D	30m	0	60
E	60m	0	60

Question 84:

An object approaches a stationary observer at a 10% of the speed of light, c. If the observer is 2 m tall, how tall will it look to the object?

A. $0.9l$

B. $1.1l$

C. l

D. $l\sqrt{0.99}$

E. $l\sqrt{1.01}$

Question 85:

What is the stopping distance of a car moving at v m/s if its breaking force is half its weight?

A. v^2

B. $\frac{v^2}{g}$

C. $2mv$

D. $\frac{v^2}{2}$

E. $\sqrt{mg}$

Question 86:

The amplitude of a wave is damped from an initial amplitude of 200 to 25 over 12 seconds. How many seconds did it take to reach half its original amplitude?

A. 1
B. 2
C. 3
D. 4
E. 6

Question 87:

Two frequencies, f and $\frac{7}{8}f$, interfere to produce beats of 10 Hz. What is the original frequency f?

A. 11 Hz
B. 60 Hz
C. 80 Hz
D. 160 Hz
E. 200 Hz

Question 88:

Refer to the diagram opposite. The two waves represent:

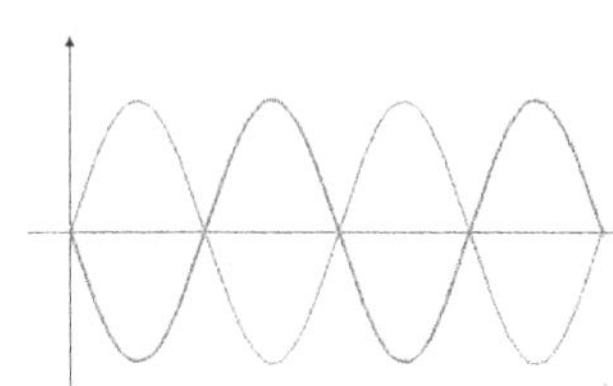

A. A standing wave with both ends fixed
B. The 4th harmonic
C. Destructive interference
D. A reflection from a plane surface
E. All of the above

Question 89:

Radioactive element ${}^{a}_{b}X$ undergoes beta decay, and the product of this decay emits an alpha particle to become ${}^{c}_{d}Y$. What are the atomic number and atomic mass?

	c	d
A	a-4	b+1
B	a-3	b-2
C	a-4	b-1
D	a-5	b
E	a-1	b-4

Question 90:

A gas is heated to twice its temperature (in Kelvin) and allowed to increase in volume by 10%. What is the change in pressure?

A. 82% increase
B. 90% increase
C. 110% increase
D. 18% decrease
E. 40% decrease
F. 82% decrease

Question 91:

A beam of alpha particles enters perpendicular to the magnetic field, B, shown below coming out of the page and is deflected to follow path T. What path would a beam of electrons follow?

A. P
B. Q
C. R
D. S

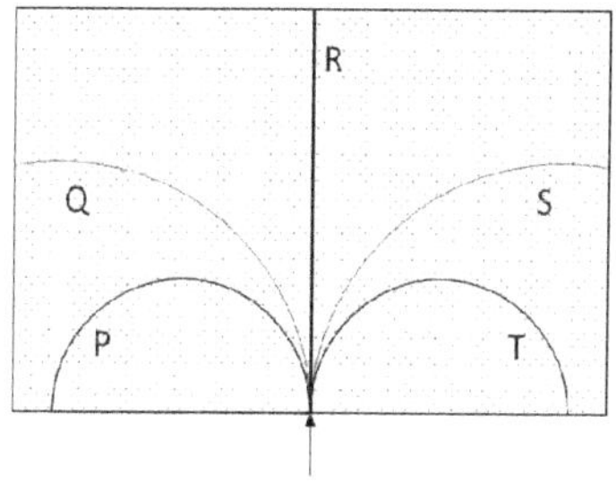

Question 92:

If all light bulbs and power supplies are identical and the joining wires have negligible resistance, which of the following light bulbs will shine brightest?

A. 1,2,3
B. 6
C. 7,8,9
D. 1,2,3,6
E. 4,5

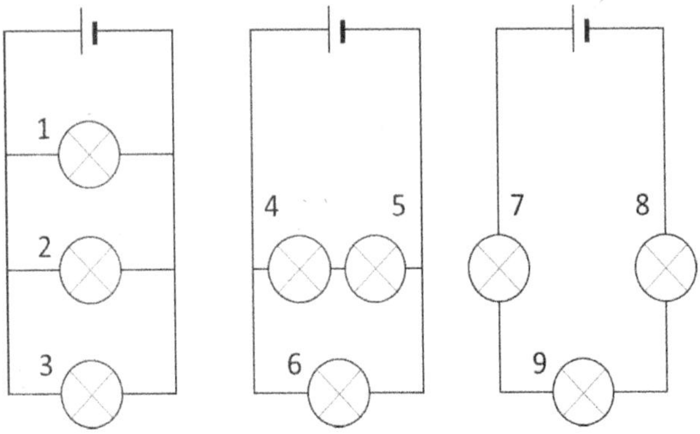

Question 93:

A convex lens with focal length f is used to create an image of object O. Where is the image formed?

A. V
B. W
C. X
D. Y
E. Z

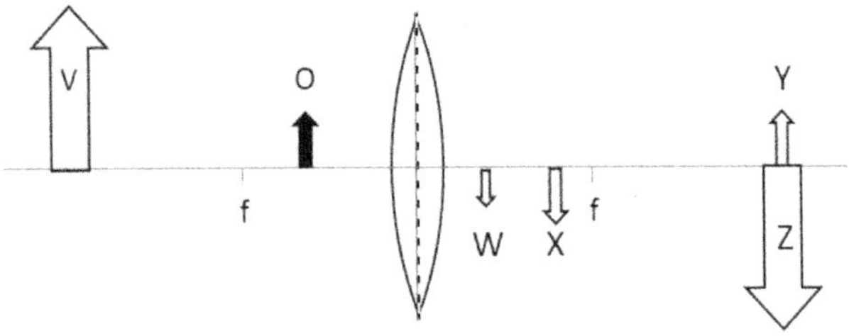

Question 94:

A flower pot hangs on the end of a rod protruding at right angles from a wall, held up by string attached two thirds of the way along. What must the tension in the string be if the rod is weightless and the system is at equilibrium?

A. $mg \sin\theta$

B. $\frac{3mg}{2\sin\theta}$

C. $\frac{3mg}{2\cos\theta}$

D. $\frac{2mg}{3\sin\theta}$

E. $\frac{2mg}{3\cos\theta}$

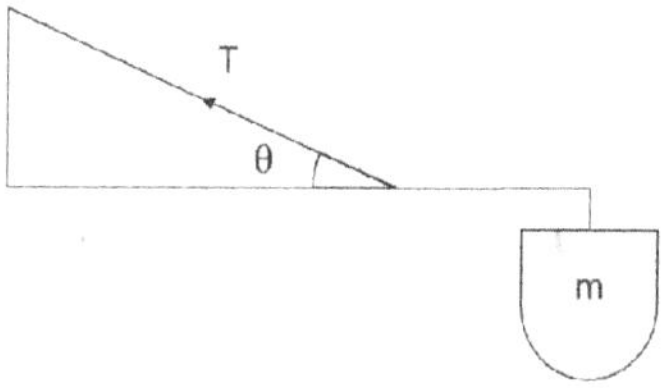

Question 95:

When a clean, negatively charged metal surface is irradiated with electromagnetic radiation of sufficient frequency, electrons are emitted. This observation describes what phenomenon and what property does the intercept on the experimental plot below represent?

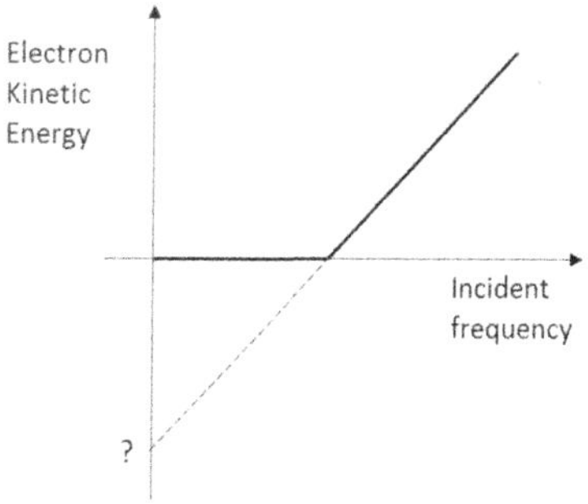

A	Photoelectric effect	Stopping potential
B	Evaporation	Stopping potential
C	Wave particle duality	Work function
D	Thermionic emission	Work function
E	Photoabsorbtion	Stopping potential

Question 96:
Which of these wave phenomena can be explained by Huygen's principle of wave propagation?

1. Diffraction
2. Refraction
3. Reflection
4. Interference
5. Damping

A. None
B. 1,2,3
C. 1,4
D. 1,2,3,4
E. All

Question 97:
What is the maximum efficiency of an engine where the isothermal expansion of a gas takes place at $T_1 = 420$ K and the reversible isothermal compression of the gas occurs at temperature $T_2 = 280$ K?

A. 43%
B. 57%
C. 75%
D. 92%
E. 100%

Question 98:
Which of the following statements is true?

A. A capacitor works based on the principle of electromagnetic induction.
B. A motor requires a AC input
C. Transformers produce DC current
D. The magnetic field produced by a current carrying wire is parallel to the direction of flow of charge.
E. A generator must have a moving wire.

Question 99:

For the logic gate below, if inputs are all set to 1, what would the value of X, Y and Z be?

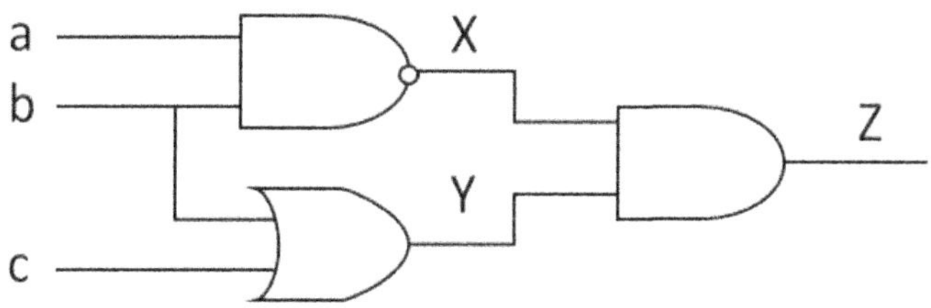

	X	Y	Z
A	0	0	0
B	0	0	1
C	0	1	0
D	1	0	0
E	1	1	1

Question 100:
What material property is given by each point P, Q and R on a stress-strain curve?

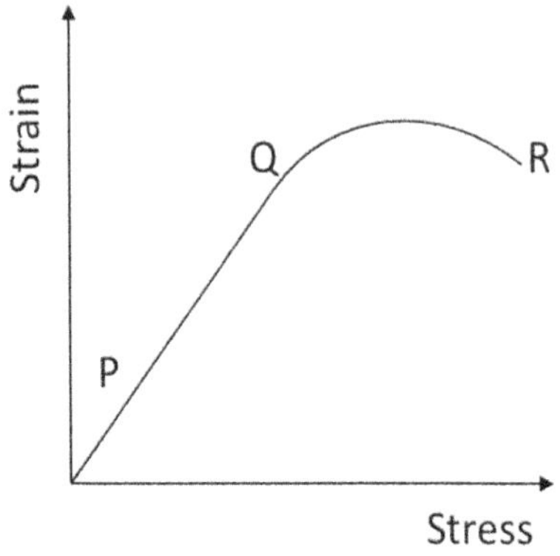

	P	Q	R
A	Elastic Modulus	Yield stress	Fracture toughness
B	Tensile Modulus	Plastic onset	Yield stress
C	Hardness	Stiffness	Ductile failure
D	Ductility	Elastic limit	Brittle fracture
E	Young's Modulus	Yield stress	Fracture stress

SECTION 1: Maths

Advanced Maths Syllabus

Algebra:

- Laws of Indices
- Manipulation of Surds
- Quadratic Functions: Graphs, use of discriminant, completing the square
- Solving Simultaneous Equations via Substitution
- Solving Linear and Quadratic Inequalities
- Manipulation of polynomials e.g. expanding brackets, factorising
- Use of Factor Theorem + Remainder Theorem

Graphing Functions:

- Sketching of common functions including lines, quadratics, cubics, trigonometric functions, logarithmic functions and exponential functions
- Manipulation of functions using simple transformations

Differentiation:

- First order and second order derivatives
- Familiarity with notation: $\frac{dy}{dx}, \frac{d^2y}{dx^2}, f'(x), f''(x)$
- Differentiation of functions like $y = x^n$

Integration:

- Definite and indefinite integrals for $y = x^n$
- Solving Differential Equations in the form: $\frac{dy}{dx} = f(x)$
- Understanding of the Fundamental Theorem of Calculus and its application:
  - $\int_a^b f(x)dx = F(b) - F(a), where\ F'(x) = f(x)$

- $\frac{d}{dx}\int_a^x f(t)dt = f(x)$

Geometry:

- Circle Properties:
  - The angle subtended by an arc at the centre of a circle is double the size of the angle subtended by the arc on the circumference
  - The opposite angles in a cyclic quadrilateral summate to 180 degrees
  - The angle between the tangent and chord at the point of contact is equal to the angle in the alternate segment
  - The tangent at any point on a circle is perpendicular to the radius at that point
  - Triangles formed using the full diameter are right-angled triangles
  - Angles in the same segment are equal
  - The Perpendicular from the centre to a chord bisects the chord
- Equations for a circle:
  - $(x-a)^2 + (y-b)^2 = r^2$
  - $x^2 + y^2 + cx + dy + e = 0$
- Equations for a straight line:
  - $y - y_1 = m(x - x_1)$
  - $Ax + by + c = 0$

Series:

- Arithmetic series and Geometric series
- Summing to a finite and infinite geometric series
- Binomial Expansions
- Factorials

Trigonometry:

- Sine and Cosine rules
- Solution of trigonometric identities
- Values of sin, cost, tan for 0, 30, 45, 60 and 90 degrees

- Sine, Cosine, Tangent Graphs, Symmetries, Periodicities

Logic Arguments:

- Terminology: True, false, and, or not, necessary, sufficient, for all, for some, there exists.
- Arguments in the format:
  - If A then B
  - A if B
  - A only if B
  - A if and only if B

Law of Logarithms

- $a^b = c \leftrightarrow b = log_a c$
- $log_a x + log_a y = log_a(xy)$
- $log_a x - log_a y = log_a(\frac{x}{y})$
- $k \, log_a x = log_a(x^k)$
- $log_a \frac{1}{x} = -\, log_a x$
- $log_a a = 1$

Trigonometry

- Sin Rule: $\frac{a}{SinA} = \frac{b}{Sin\,B} = \frac{c}{Sin\,C}$
- Cosine Rule: $c^2 = a^2 + b^2 - 2ab\,cosC$
- $Area\ of\ Triangle = \frac{1}{2}ab\sin C$
- $\sin^2\theta + \cos^2\theta = 1$
- $tan\theta = \frac{sin\theta}{\cos\theta}$

Exponentials & Logs:

- Graph of $y = a^x$ series
- Law of Logarithms

Core Formulas:

2D Shapes		3D Shapes		
	Area		**Surface Area**	**Volume**
Circle	πr^2	**Cuboid**	Σ of 6 faces	Length x width x height
Parallelogram	Base x Vertical height	**Cylinder**	$2\pi r^2 + 2\pi rl$	$\pi r^2 \times l$
Trapezium	0.5 x h x (a+b)	**Cone**	$\pi r^2 + \pi rl$	$\pi r^2 \times (h/3)$
Triangle	0.5 x base x height	**Sphere**	$4\pi r^2$	$(4/3)\pi r^3$

Even good students who are studying maths at A2 can struggle with certain ENGAA maths topics because they're usually glossed over at school. These include:

Quadratic Formula

The solutions for a quadratic equation in the form $ax^2 + bx + c = 0$ are given by: $x = \frac{-b \pm \sqrt{b^2 - 4ac}}{2a}$

Remember that you can also use the discriminant to quickly see if a quadratic equation has any solutions:

$$b^2 - 4ac < 0 \Rightarrow No\ solutions$$
$$b^2 - 4ac = 0 \Rightarrow 1\ solution$$
$$b^2 - 4ac > 2 \Rightarrow 2\ solutions$$

Completing the Square

If a quadratic equation cannot be factorised easily and is in the format $ax^2 + bx + c = 0$ then you can rearrange it into the form $a\left(x + \frac{b}{2a}\right)^2 + [c - \frac{b^2}{4a}] = 0$

This looks more complicated than it is – remember that in the ENGAA, you're extremely unlikely to get quadratic equations where $a > 1$ and the equation doesn't have any easy factors. This gives you an easier equation: $\left(x + \frac{b}{2}\right)^2 + \left[c - \frac{b^2}{4}\right] = 0$ and is best understood with an example.

Consider: $x^2 + 6x + 10 = 0$

This equation cannot be factorised easily but note that: $x^2 + 6x - 10 = (x + 3)^2 - 19 = 0$

Therefore, $x = -3 \pm \sqrt{19}$. Completing the square is an important skill – make sure you're comfortable with it.

Difference between 2 Squares

If you are asked to simplify expressions and find that there are no common factors but it involves square numbers – you might be able to factorise by using the 'difference between two squares'.

For example, $x^2 - 25$ can also be expressed as $(x + 5)(x - 5)$.

Maths Questions

Question 101:

Robert has a box of building blocks. The box contains 8 yellow blocks and 12 red blocks. He picks three blocks from the box and stacks them up high. Calculate the probability that he stacks two red building blocks and one yellow building block, in **any** order.

A. $\frac{8}{20}$

B. $\frac{44}{95}$

C. $\frac{11}{18}$

D. $\frac{8}{19}$

E. $\frac{12}{20}$

F. $\frac{35}{60}$

Question 102:

Solve $\frac{3x+5}{5} + \frac{2x-2}{3} = 18$

A. 12.11

B. 13.49

C. 13.95

D. 14.2

E. 19

F. 265

Question 103:

Solve $3x^2 + 11x - 20 = 0$

A. 0.75 and $-\frac{4}{3}$

B. -0.75 and $\frac{4}{3}$

C. -5 and $\frac{4}{3}$

D. 5 and $\frac{4}{3}$

E. 12 only

F. -12 only

Question 104:

Express $\frac{5}{x+2} + \frac{3}{x-4}$ as a single fraction.

A. $\frac{15x-120}{(x+2)(x-4)}$

B. $\frac{8x-26}{(x+2)(x-4)}$

C. $\frac{8x-14}{(x+2)(x-4)}$

D. $\frac{15}{8x}$

E. 24

F. $\frac{8x-14}{x^2-8}$

Question 105:

The value of p is directly proportional to the cube root of q. When p = 12, q = 27. Find the value of q when p = 24.

A. 32
B. 64
C. 124
D. 128
E. 216
F. 1728

Question 106:

Write 72^2 as a product of its prime factors.

A. $2^6 \times 3^4$
B. $2^6 \times 3^5$
C. $2^4 \times 3^4$
D. 2×3^3
E. $2^6 \times 3$
F. $2^3 \times 3^2$

Question 107:

Calculate: $\frac{2.302 \times 10^5 + 2.302 \times 10^2}{1.151 \times 10^{10}}$

A. 0.0000202
B. 0.00020002
C. 0.00002002
D. 0.00000002
E. 0.000002002
F. 0.000002002

Question 108:

Given that $y^2 + \mathbf{a}y + \mathbf{b} = (y + 2)^2 - 5$, find the values of **a** and **b**.

	a	b
A	-1	4
B	1	9
C	-1	-9
D	-9	1
E	4	-1
F	4	1

Question 109:

Express $\frac{4}{5} + \frac{m-2n}{m+4n}$ as a single fraction in its simplest form:

A. $\frac{6m+6n}{5(m+4n)}$

B. $\frac{9m+26n}{5(m+4n)}$

C. $\frac{20m+6n}{5(m+4n)}$

D. $\frac{3m+9n}{5(m+4n)}$

E. $\frac{3(3m+2n)}{5(m+4n)}$

F. $\frac{6m+6n}{3(m+4n)}$

Question 110:

A is inversely proportional to the square root of B. When A = 4, B = 25.

Calculate the value of A when B = 16.

A. 0.8

B. 4

C. 5

D. 6

E. 10

F. 20

Question 111:

S, T, U and V are points on the circumference of a circle, and O is the centre of the circle.

Given that angle SVU = 89°, calculate the size of the smaller angle SOU.

A. 89°
B. 91°
C. 102°
D. 178°
E. 182°
F. 212°

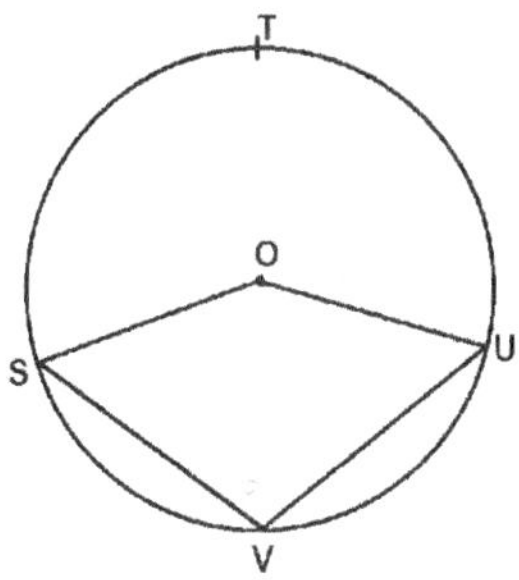

✱ **Question 112:**

Open cylinder A has a surface area of 8π cm^2 and a volume of 2π cm^3. Open cylinder B is an enlargement of A and has a surface area of 32π cm^2. Calculate the volume of cylinder B.

A. 2π cm^3
B. 8π cm^3
C. 10π cm^3
D. 14π cm^3
E. 16π cm^3
F. 32π cm^3

Question 113:

Express $\frac{8}{x(3-x)} - \frac{6}{x}$ in its simplest form.

A. $\frac{3x-10}{x(3-x)}$
B. $\frac{3x+10}{x(3-x)}$
C. $\frac{6x-10}{x(3-2x)}$
D. $\frac{6x-10}{x(3+2x)}$
E. $\frac{6x-10}{x(3-x)}$
F. $\frac{6x+10}{x(3-x)}$

Question 114:

A bag contains 10 balls. 9 of those are white and 1 is black. What is the probability that the black ball is drawn in the tenth and final draw if the drawn balls are not replaced?

A. 0

B. $\frac{1}{10}$

C. $\frac{1}{100}$

D. $\frac{1}{10^{10}}$

E. $\frac{1}{362,880}$

Question 115:

Gambit has an ordinary deck of 52 cards. What is the probability of Gambit drawing 2 Kings (without replacement)?

A. 0

B. $\frac{1}{169}$

C. $\frac{1}{221}$

D. $\frac{4}{663}$

E. None of the above

Question 116:

I have two identical unfair dice, where the probability that the dice get a 6 is twice as high as the probability of any other outcome, which are all equally likely. What is the probability that when I roll both dice the total will be 12?

A. 0

B. $\frac{4}{49}$

C. $\frac{1}{9}$

D. $\frac{2}{7}$

E. None of the above

Question 117:

A roulette wheel consists of 36 numbered spots and 1 zero spot (i.e. 37 spots in total).

What is the probability that the ball will stop in a spot either divisible by 3 or 2?

A. 0

B. $\frac{25}{37}$

C. $\frac{25}{36}$

D. $\frac{18}{37}$

E. $\frac{24}{37}$

Question 118:

I have a fair coin that I flip 4 times. What is the probability I get 2 heads and 2 tails?

A. $\frac{1}{16}$

B. $\frac{3}{16}$

C. $\frac{3}{8}$

D. $\frac{9}{16}$

E. None of the above

Question 119:

Shivun rolls two fair dice. What is the probability that he gets a total of 5, 6 or 7?

A. $\frac{9}{36}$

B. $\frac{7}{12}$

C. $\frac{1}{6}$

D. $\frac{5}{12}$

E. None of the above

Question 120:

Dr Savary has a bag that contains x red balls, y blue balls and z green balls (and no others). He pulls out a ball, replaces it, and then pulls out another. What is the probability that he picks one red ball and one green ball?

A. $\frac{2(x+y)}{x+y+z}$

B. $\frac{xz}{(x+y+z)^2}$

C. $\frac{2xz}{(x+y+z)^2}$

D. $\frac{(x+z)}{(x+y+z)^2}$

E. $\frac{4xz}{(x+y+z)^4}$

F. More information necessary

Question 121:

Mr Kilbane has a bag that contains x red balls, y blue balls and z green balls (and no others). He pulls out a ball, does **NOT** replace it, and then pulls out another. What is the probability that he picks one red ball and one blue ball?

A. $\frac{2xy}{(x+y+z)^2}$

B. $\frac{2xy}{(x+y+z)(x+y+z-1)}$

C. $\frac{2xy}{(x+y+z)^2}$

D. $\frac{xy}{(x+y+z)(x+y+z-1)}$

E. $\frac{4xy}{(x+y+z-1)^2}$

F. More information needed

Question 122:

There are two tennis players. The first player wins the point with probability p, and the second player wins the point with probability 1-p. The rules of tennis say that the first player to score four points wins the game, unless the score is 4-3. At this point the first player to get two points ahead wins.

What is the probability that the first player wins in exactly 5 rounds?

A. $4p^4(1-p)$
B. $p^4(1-p)$
C. $4p(1-p)$
D. $4p(1-p)^4$
E. $4p^5(1-p)$
F. More information needed.

Question 123:

Solve the equation $\frac{4x+7}{2} + 9x + 10 = 7$

A. $\frac{22}{13}$
B. $-\frac{22}{13}$
C. $\frac{10}{13}$
D. $-\frac{10}{13}$
E. $\frac{13}{22}$
F. $-\frac{13}{22}$

Question 124:

The volume of a sphere is $V = \frac{4}{3}\pi r^3$, and the surface area of a sphere is $S = 4\pi r^2$. Express S in terms of V

A. $S = (4\pi)^{2/3}(3V)^{2/3}$
B. $S = (8\pi)^{1/3}(3V)^{2/3}$
C. $S = (4\pi)^{1/3}(9V)^{2/3}$
D. $S = (4\pi)^{1/3}(3V)^{2/3}$
E. $S = (16\pi)^{1/3}(9V)^{2/3}$

Question 125:

Express the volume of a cube, *V*, in terms of its surface area, *S*.

A. $V = (S/6)^{3/2}$
B. $V = S^{3/2}$
C. $V = (6/S)^{3/2}$
D. $V = (S/6)^{1/2}$
E. $V = (S/36)^{1/2}$
F. $V = (S/36)^{3/2}$

Question 126:

Solve the equations $4x + 3y = 7$ and $2x + 8y = 12$

A. $(x,y) = \left(\frac{17}{13}, \frac{10}{13}\right)$
B. $(x,y) = \left(\frac{10}{13}, \frac{17}{13}\right)$
C. $(x,y) = (1,2)$
D. $(x,y) = (2,1)$
E. $(x,y) = (6,3)$
F. $(x,y) = (3,6)$
G. No solutions possible.

Question 127:

Rearrange $\frac{(7x+10)}{(9x+5)} = 3y^2 + 2$, to make x the subject.

A. $\frac{15y^2}{7-9(3y^2+2)}$
B. $\frac{15y^2}{7+9(3y^2+2)}$
C. $-\frac{15y^2}{7-9(3y^2+2)}$
D. $-\frac{15y^2}{7+9(3y^2+2)}$
E. $-\frac{5y^2}{7+9(3y^2+2)}$
F. $\frac{5y^2}{7+9(3y^2+2)}$

Question 128:

Simplify $3x\left(\frac{3x^7}{x^{\frac{1}{3}}}\right)^3$

A. $9x^{20}$

B. $27x^{20}$

C. $87x^{20}$

D. $9x^{21}$

E. $27x^{21}$

F. $81x^{21}$

Question 129:

Simplify $2x[(2x)^7]^{\frac{1}{14}}$

$2x\sqrt{2x}$

A. $2x\sqrt{2\,x^4}$

B. $2x\sqrt{2x^3}$

C. $2\sqrt{2\,x^4}$

D. $2\sqrt{2x^3}$

E. $8x^3$

F. $8x$

Question 130:

What is the circumference of a circle with an area of 10π?

A. $2\pi\sqrt{10}$

B. $\pi\sqrt{10}$

C. 10π

D. 20π

E. $\sqrt{10}$

F. More information needed.

Question 131:

If $a.b = (ab) + (a + b)$, then calculate the value of $(3.4).5$

A. 19

B. 54

C. 100

D. 119

E. 132

Question 132:

If $a.b = \frac{a^b}{a}$, calculate(2.3).2

A. $\frac{16}{3}$

B. 1

C. 2

D. 4

E. 8

Question 133:

Solve $x^2 + 3x - 5 = 0$

A. $x = -\frac{3}{2} \pm \frac{\sqrt{11}}{2}$

B. $x = \frac{3}{2} \pm \frac{\sqrt{11}}{2}$

C. $x = -\frac{3}{2} \pm \frac{\sqrt{11}}{4}$

D. $x = \frac{3}{2} \pm \frac{\sqrt{11}}{4}$

E. $x = \frac{3}{2} \pm \frac{\sqrt{29}}{2}$

F. $x = -\frac{3}{2} \pm \frac{\sqrt{29}}{2}$

Question 134:

How many times do the curves $y = x^3$ and $y = x^2 + 4x + 14$ intersect?

A. 0

B. 1

C. 2

D. 3

E. 4

Question 135:

Which of the following graphs **do not** intersect?

1. $y = x$
2. $y = x^2$
3. $y = 1-x^2$
4. $y = 2$

A. 1 and 2
B. 2 and 3
C. 3 and 4
D. 1 and 3
E. 1 and 4
F. 2 and 4

Question 136:

Calculate the product of 897,653 and 0.009764.

A. 87646.8
B. 8764.68
C. 876.468
D. 87.6468
E. 8.76468
F. 0.876468

Question 137:

Solve for x: $\frac{7x+3}{10} + \frac{3x+1}{7} = 14$

A. $\frac{929}{51}$
B. $\frac{949}{47}$
C. $\frac{949}{79}$
D. $\frac{980}{79}$

Question 138:

What is the area of an equilateral triangle with side length x.

A. $\frac{x^2\sqrt{3}}{4}$

B. $\frac{x\sqrt{3}}{4}$

C. $\frac{x^2}{2}$

D. $\frac{x}{2}$

E. x^2

F. x

Question 139:

Simplify $3 - \frac{7x(25x^2 - 1)}{49x^2(5x+1)}$

A. $3 - \frac{5x-1}{7x}$

B. $3 - \frac{5x+1}{7x}$

C. $3 + \frac{5x-1}{7x}$

D. $3 + \frac{5x+1}{7x}$

E. $3 - \frac{5x^2}{49}$

F. $3 + \frac{5x^2}{49}$

Question 140:

Solve the equation $x^2 - 10x - 100 = 0$

A. $-5 \pm 5\sqrt{5}$

B. $-5 \pm \sqrt{5}$

C. $5 \pm 5\sqrt{5}$

D. $5 \pm \sqrt{5}$

E. $5 \pm 5\sqrt{125}$

F. $-5 \pm \sqrt{125}$

Question 141:

Rearrange $x^2 - 4x + 7 = y^3 + 2$ to make x the subject.

A. $x = 2 \pm \sqrt{y^3 + 1}$

B. $x = 2 \pm \sqrt{y^3 - 1}$

C. $x = -2 \pm \sqrt{y^3 - 1}$

D. $x = -2 \pm \sqrt{y^3 + 1}$

E. x cannot be made the subject for this equation.

Question 142:

Rearrange $3x + 2 = \sqrt{7x^2 + 2x + y}$ to make y the subject.

A. $y = 4x^2 + 8x + 2$

B. $y = 4x^2 + 8x + 4$

C. $y = 2x^2 + 10x + 2$

D. $y = 2x^2 + 10x + 4$

E. $y = x^2 + 10x + 2$

F. $y = x^2 + 10x + 4$

Question 143:

Rearrange $y^4 - 4y^3 + 6y^2 - 4y + 2 = x^5 + 7$ to make y the subject.

A. $y = 1 + (x^5 + 7)^{1/4}$

B. $y = -1 + (x^5 + 7)^{1/4}$

C. $y = 1 + (x^5 + 6)^{1/4}$

D. $y = -1 + (x^5 + 6)^{1/4}$

Question 144:

The aspect ratio of my television screen is 4:3 and the diagonal is 50 inches. What is the area of my television screen?

A. 1,200 inches^2

B. 1,000 inches^2

C. 120 inches^2

D. 100 inches^2

E. More information needed.

Question 145:

Rearrange the equation $\sqrt{1 + 3x^{-2}} = y^5 + 1$ to make x the subject.

A. $x = \frac{(y^{10} + 2y^5)}{3}$

B. $x = \frac{3}{(y^{10} + 2y^5)}$

C. $x = \sqrt{\frac{3}{y^{10} + 2y^5}}$

D. $x = \sqrt{\frac{y^{10} + 2y^5}{3}}$

E. $x = \sqrt{\frac{y^{10} + 2y^5 + 2}{3}}$

F. $x = \sqrt{\frac{3}{y^{10} + 2y^5 + 2}}$

Question 146:

Solve $3x - 5y = 10 \; and \; 2x + 2y = 13$.

A. $(x,y) = (\frac{19}{16}, \frac{85}{16})$

B. $(x,y) = (\frac{85}{16}, -\frac{19}{16})$

C. $(x,y) = (\frac{85}{16}, \frac{19}{16})$

D. $(x,y) = (-\frac{85}{16}, -\frac{19}{16})$

E. No solutions possible.

Question 147:

The two inequalities $x + y \leq 3 \; and \; x^3 - y^2 < 3$ define a region on a plane. Which of the following points is inside the region?

A. (2, 1)

B. (2.5, 1)

C. (1, 2)

D. (3, 5)

E. (1, 2.5)

F. None of the above.

Question 148:

How many times do $y = x + 4 \; and \; y = 4x^2 + 5x + 5$ intersect?

A. 0

B. 1

C. 2

D. 3

E. 4

Question 149:

How many times do $y = x^3$ *and* $y = x$ intersect?

A. 0

B. 1

C. 2

D. 3

E. 4

Question 150:

A cube has unit length sides. What is the length of a line joining a vertex to the midpoint of the opposite side?

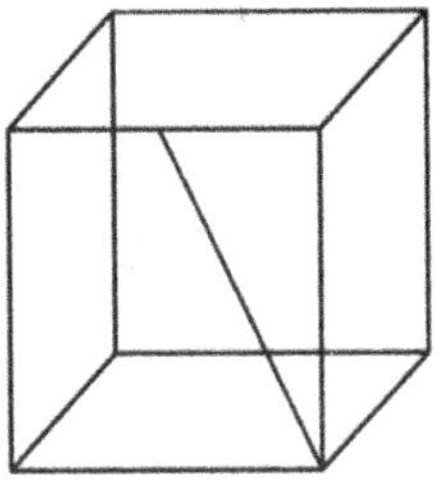

A. $\sqrt{2}$

B. $\sqrt{\frac{3}{2}}$

C. $\sqrt{3}$

D. $\sqrt{5}$

E. $\frac{\sqrt{5}}{2}$

Question 151:

Solve for x, y, and z.

1. $x + y - z = -1$
2. $2x - 2y + 3z = 8$
3. $2x - y + 2z = 9$

	x	y	z
A	2	-15	-14
B	15	2	14
C	14	15	-2
D	-2	15	14
E	2	-15	14
F	No solutions possible		

Question 152:

Fully factorise: $3a^3 - 30a^2 + 75a$

A. $3a(a-3)^3$

B. $a(3a-5)^2$

C. $3a(a^2 - 10a + 25)$

D. $3a(a-5)^2$

E. $3a(a+5)^2$

Question 153:

Solve for x and y:

$$4x + 3y = 48$$
$$3x + 2y = 34$$

	x	y
A	8	6
B	6	8
C	3	4
D	4	3
E	30	12
F	12	30
G	No solutions possible	

Question 154:

Evaluate: $\frac{-(5^2-4 \times 7)^2}{-6^2+2 \times 7}$

A. $-\frac{3}{50}$

B. $\frac{11}{22}$

C. $-\frac{3}{22}$

D. $\frac{9}{50}$

E. $\frac{9}{22}$

F. 0

Question 155:

All license plates are 6 characters long. The first 3 characters consist of letters and the next 3 characters of numbers. How many unique license plates are possible?

A. 676,000

B. 6,760,000

C. 67,600,000

D. 1,757,600

E. 17,576,000

F. 175,760,000

Question 156:

How many solutions are there for: $2(2(x^2 - 3x)) = -9$

A. 0

B. 1

C. 2

D. 3

E. Infinite solutions.

Question 157:

Evaluate: $\left(x^{\frac{1}{2}} y^{-3}\right)^{\frac{1}{2}}$

A. $\frac{x^{\frac{1}{2}}}{y}$

B. $\frac{x}{y^{\frac{3}{2}}}$

C. $\frac{x^{\frac{1}{4}}}{y^{\frac{3}{2}}}$

D. $\frac{y^{\frac{1}{4}}}{x^{\frac{3}{2}}}$

Question 158:

Bryan earned a total of £ 1,240 last week from renting out three flats. From this, he had to pay 10% of the rent from the 1-bedroom flat for repairs, 20% of the rent from the 2-bedroom flat for repairs, and 30% from the 3-bedroom flat for repairs. The 3-bedroom flat costs twice as much as the 1-bedroom flat. Given that the total repair bill was £ 276 calculate the rent for each apartment.

	1 Bedroom	2 Bedrooms	3 Bedrooms
A	280	400	560
B	140	200	280
C	420	600	840
D	250	300	500
E	500	600	1,000

Question 159:

Evaluate: $5\,[5(6^2 - 5 \times 3) + 400^{\frac{1}{2}}]^{1/3} + 7$

A. 0
B. 25
C. 32
D. 49
E. 56
F. 200

Question 160:

What is the area of a regular hexagon with side length 1?

A. $3\sqrt{3}$

B. $\frac{3\sqrt{3}}{2}$

C. $\sqrt{3}$

D. $\frac{\sqrt{3}}{2}$

E. 6

F. More information needed

Question 161:

Dexter moves into a new rectangular room that is 19 metres longer than it is wide, and its total area is 780 square metres. What are the room's dimensions?

A. Width = 20 m; Length = -39 m
B. Width = 20 m; Length = 39 m
C. Width = 39 m; Length = 20 m
D. Width = -39 m; Length = 20 m
E. Width = -20 m; Length = 39 m

Question 162:

Tom uses 34 meters of fencing to enclose his rectangular lot. He measured the diagonals to 13 metres long. What is the length and width of the lot?

A. 3 m by 4 m

B. 5 m by 12 m

C. 6 m by 12 m

D. 8 m by 15 m

E. 9 m by 15 m

F. 10 m by 10 m

Question 163:

Solve $\frac{3x-5}{2} + \frac{x+5}{4} = x + 1$

A. 1
B. 1.5
C. 3
D. 3.5
E. 4.5
F. None of the above

Question 164:

Calculate: $\frac{5.226 \text{ x } 10^6 + 5.226 \text{ x } 10^5}{1.742 \text{ x } 10^{10}}$

A. 0.033
B. 0.0033
C. 0.00033
D. 0.000033
E. 0.0000033

Question 165:

Calculate the area of the triangle shown to the right:

A. $3 + \sqrt{2}$
B. $\frac{2 + 2\sqrt{2}}{2}$
C. $2 + 5\sqrt{2}$
D. $3 - \sqrt{2}$
E. 3
F. 6

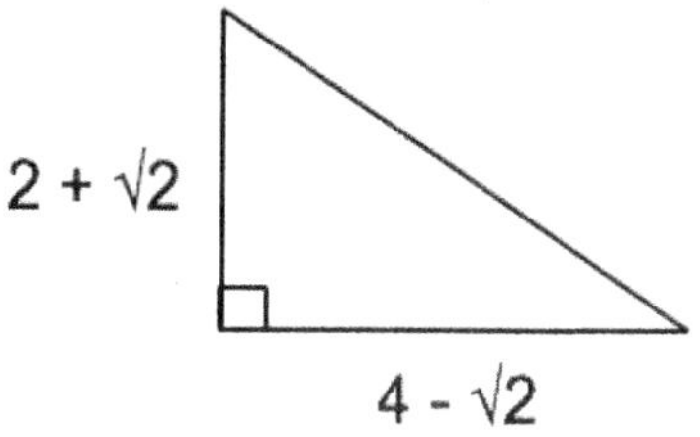

Question 166:

Rearrange $\sqrt{\frac{4}{x}+9} = y-2$ to make x the subject.

A. $x = \frac{11}{(y-2)^2}$

B. $x = \frac{9}{(y-2)^2}$

C. $x = \frac{4}{(y+1)(y-5)}$

D. $x = \frac{4}{(y-1)(y+5)}$

E. $x = \frac{4}{(y+1)(y+5)}$

F. $x = \frac{4}{(y-1)(y-5)}$

Question 167:

When 5 is subtracted from 5x the result is half the sum of 2 and 6x. What is the value of x?

A. 0

B. 1

C. 2

D. 3

E. 4

F. 6

Question 168:

Estimate $\frac{54.98 + 2.25^2}{\sqrt{905}}$

A. 0

B. 1

C. 2

D. 3

E. 4

F. 5

Question 169:

At a Pizza Parlour, you can order single, double or triple cheese in the crust. You also have the option to include ham, olives, pepperoni, bell pepper, meat balls, tomato slices, and pineapples. How many different types of pizza are available at the Pizza Parlour?

A. 10
B. 96
C. 192
D. 384
E. 768
F. None of the above

Question 170:

Solve the simultaneous equations $x^2 + y^2 = 1$ and $x + y = \sqrt{2}$, for x, y > 0

A. $(x, y) = (\frac{\sqrt{2}}{2}, \frac{\sqrt{2}}{2})$
B. $(x, y) = (½, \frac{\sqrt{3}}{2})$
C. $(x, y) = (\sqrt{2} - 1, 1)$
D. $(x, y) = (\sqrt{2}, ½)$

Question 171:

Which of the following statements is **FALSE**?

A. Congruent objects always have the same dimensions and shape.
B. Congruent objects can be mirror images of each other.
C. Congruent objects do not always have the same angles.
D. Congruent objects can be rotations of each other.
E. Two triangles are congruent if they have two sides and one angle of the same magnitude.

Question 172:

Solve the inequality $x^2 \geq 6 - x$

A. $x \leq -3$ and $x \leq 2$

B. $x \leq -3$ and $x \geq 2$

C. $x \geq -3$ and $x \leq 2$

D. $x \geq -3$ and $x \geq 2$

E. $x \geq 2$ only

F. $x \geq -3$ only

Question 173:

The hypotenuse of an equilateral right-angled triangle is x cm. What is the area of the triangle in terms of x?

A. $\frac{\sqrt{x}}{2}$ B. $\frac{x^2}{4}$ C. $\frac{x}{4}$ D. $\frac{3x^2}{4}$ E. $\frac{x^2}{10}$

Question 174:

Mr Heard derives a formula: $Q = \frac{(X+Y)^2 A}{3B}$. He doubles the values of X and Y, halves the value of A and triples the value of B. What happens to value of Q?

A. Decreases by $\frac{1}{3}$

B. Increases by $\frac{1}{3}$

C. Decreases by $\frac{2}{3}$

D. Increases by $\frac{2}{3}$

E. Increases by $\frac{4}{3}$

F. Decreases by $\frac{4}{3}$

Question 175:

Consider the graphs $y = x^2 - 2x + 3$, and $y = x^2 - 6x - 10$. Which of the following is true?

A. Both equations intersect the x-axis.

B. Neither equation intersects the x-axis.

C. The first equation does not intersect the x-axis; the second equation intersects the x-axis.

D. The first equation intersects the x-axis; the second equation does not intersect the x-axis.

Advanced Maths Questions

Question 176:

The vertex of an equilateral triangle is covered by a circle whose radius is half the height of the triangle. What percentage of the triangle is covered by the circle?

A. 12%

B. 16%

C. 23% ✓

D. 33%

E. 41%

F. 50%

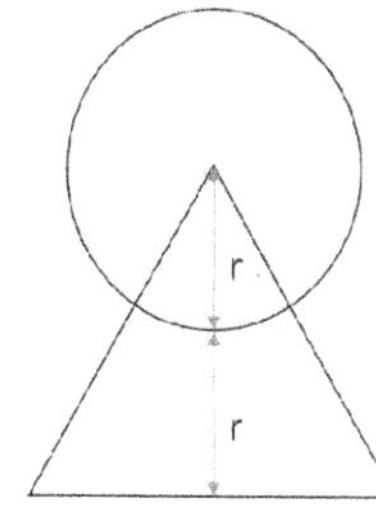

Question 177:

Three equal circles fit into a quadrilateral as shown, what is the height of the quadrilateral?

A. $2\sqrt{3}r$

B. $(2+\sqrt{3})r$ ✓

C. $(4-\sqrt{3})r$

D. $3r$

E. $4r$

F. More Information Needed

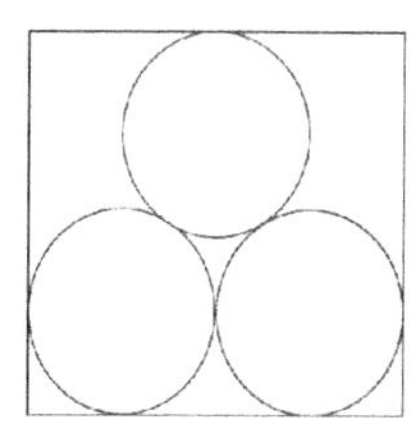

Question 178:

Two pyramids have equal volume and height, one with a square of side length ***a*** and one with a hexagonal base of side length ***b***. What is the ratio of the side length of the bases?

A. $\sqrt{\frac{3\sqrt{3}}{2}}$

B. $\sqrt{\frac{2\sqrt{3}}{3}}$

C. $\sqrt{\frac{3}{2}}$

D. $\frac{2\sqrt{3}}{3}$

E. $\frac{3\sqrt{3}}{2}$

Question 179:

One 9 cm cube is cut into 3 cm cubes. The total surface area increases by a factor of:

A. $\frac{1}{3}$

B. $\sqrt{3}$

C. 3

D. 9

E. 27

Question 180:

A cone has height twice its base width (four times the circle radius). What is the cone angle (half the angle at the vertex)?

A. $30°$

B. $\sin^{-1}\left(\frac{r}{2}\right)$

C. $\sin^{-1}\left(\frac{1}{\sqrt{17}}\right)$

D. $\cos^{-1}(\sqrt{17})$

Question 181:

A hemispherical speedometer has a maximum speed of 200 mph. What is the angle travelled by the needle at a speed of 70 mph?

A. 28°
B. 49°
C. 63°
D. 88°
E. 92°

Question 182:

Two rhombuses, A and B, are similar. The area of A is 10 times that of B. What is the ratio of the smallest angles over the ratio of the shortest sides?

A. 0
B. $\frac{1}{10}$
C. $\frac{1}{\sqrt{10}}$
D. $\sqrt{10}$
E. ∞

Question 183:

$If\ f^{-1}(-x) = \ln(2x^2)$ what is $f(x)$

A. $\sqrt{\frac{e^y}{2}}$
B. $\sqrt{\frac{e^{-y}}{2}}$
C. $\frac{e^y}{2}$
D. $\frac{-e^y}{2}$
E. $\sqrt{\frac{e^y}{2}}$

Question 184:

Which of the following is largest for $0 < x < 1$

A. $log_8(x)$

B. $log_{10}(x)$

C. e^x

D. x^2

E. $\sin(x)$

Question 185:

x is proportional to y cubed, y is proportional to the square root of z. $x \propto y^3, y \propto \sqrt{z}$.

If z doubles, x changes by a factor of:

A. $\sqrt{2}$

B. 2

C. $2\sqrt{2}$

D. $\sqrt[3]{4}$

E. 4

Question 186:

The area between two concentric circles (shaded) is three times that of the inner circle.

What's the size of the gap?

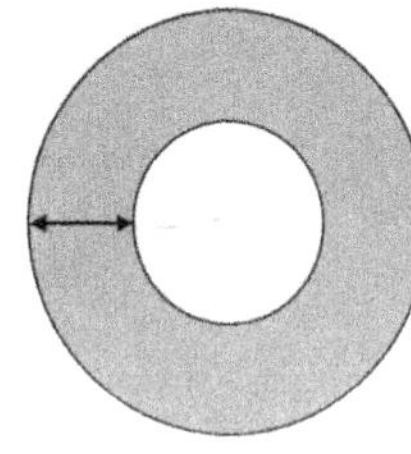

A. r

B. $\sqrt{2}r$

C. $\sqrt{3}r$

D. $2r$

E. $3r$

F. $4r$

Question 187:

Solve $-x^2 \leq 3x - 4$

A. $x \geq \frac{4}{3}$

B. $1 \leq x \leq 4$

C. $x \leq 2$

D. $x \geq 1$ or $x \geq -4$

E. $-1 \leq x \leq \frac{3}{4}$

Question 188:

The volume of a sphere is numerically equal to its projected area. What is its radius?

A. $\frac{1}{2}$

B. $\frac{2}{3}$

C. $\frac{3}{4}$

D. $\frac{4}{3}$

E. $\frac{3}{2}$

Question 189:

What is the range where $x^2 < \frac{1}{x}$?

A. $x < 0$

B. $0 < x < 1$

C. $x > 0$

D. $x \geq 1$

E. *None*

Question 190:

Simplify and solve: (e - a) (e + b) (e – c) (e + d)...(e - z)?

A. 0
B. e^{26}
C. e^{26} (a-b+c-d...+z)
D. e^{26} (a+b-c+d...-z)
E. e^{26} (abcd...z)
F. None of the above.

Question 191:

Find the value of k such that the vectors $a = -\boldsymbol{i} + 6\boldsymbol{j}$ and $b = 2\boldsymbol{i} + k\boldsymbol{j}$ are perpendicular.

A. -2
B. $-\frac{1}{3}$
C. $\frac{1}{3}$
D. 2

Question 192:

What is the perpendicular distance between point $\boldsymbol{p}$ with position vector $4\boldsymbol{i} + 5\boldsymbol{j}$ and the line L given by vector equation $\boldsymbol{r} = -3\boldsymbol{i} + \boldsymbol{j} + \lambda(\boldsymbol{i} + 2\boldsymbol{j})$

A. $2\sqrt{7}$
B. $5\sqrt{2}$
C. $2\sqrt{5}$
D. $7\sqrt{2}$

Question 193:

Find k such that point $\begin{pmatrix} 2 \\ k \\ -7 \end{pmatrix}$ lies within the plane $\boldsymbol{r} = \begin{pmatrix} 2 \\ 3 \\ -1 \end{pmatrix} + \lambda \begin{pmatrix} 4 \\ 1 \\ 0 \end{pmatrix} + \mu \begin{pmatrix} 2 \\ 1 \\ 3 \end{pmatrix}$

A. -2
B. -1
C. *0*
D. *1*
E. *2*

Question 194:

What is the largest solution to $\sin(-2\theta) = 0.5$ for $\frac{\pi}{2} \leq x \leq 2\pi$?

A. $\frac{5\pi}{3}$
B. $\frac{4\pi}{3}$
C. $\frac{5\pi}{6}$
D. $\frac{7\pi}{6}$
E. $\frac{11\pi}{6}$

Question 195:

$\cos^4(x) - \sin^4(x) \equiv$

A. $cos(2x)$
B. $2\,cos(x)$
C. $sin(2x)$
D. $sin(x)cos(x)$
E. $tan(x)$

Question 196:

How many real roots does $y = 2x^5 - 3x^4 + x^3 - 4x^2 - 6x + 4$ have?

A. *1*
B. *2*
C. *3*
D. *4*
E. *5*

Question 197:

What is the sum of 8 terms, $\sum_1^8 u_n$, of an arithmetic progression with $u_1 = 2$ and $d = 3$.

A. 15
B. 82
C. 100
D. 184
E. 282

Question 198:

What is the coefficient of the x^2 term in the binomial expansion of $(2 - x)^5$?

A. -80
B. -48
C. 40
D. 48
E. 80

Question 199:

Given you have already thrown a 6, what is the probability of throwing three consecutive 6s using a fair die?

A. $\frac{1}{216}$
B. $\frac{1}{36}$
C. $\frac{1}{6}$
D. $\frac{1}{2}$
E. *1*

Question 200:

Three people, A, B and C play darts. The probability that they hit a bull's eye are respectively $\frac{1}{5}, \frac{1}{4}, \frac{1}{3}$. What is the probability that at least two shots hit the bullseye?

A. $\frac{1}{60}$
B. $\frac{1}{30}$
C. $\frac{1}{12}$
D. $\frac{1}{6}$
E. $\frac{3}{20}$

Question 201:

If probability of having blonde hair is 1 in 4, the probability of having brown eyes is 1 in 2 and the probability of having both is 1 in 8, what is the probability of having neither blonde hair nor brown eyes?

A. $\frac{1}{2}$
B. $\frac{3}{4}$
C. $\frac{3}{8}$
D. $\frac{5}{8}$
E. $\frac{7}{8}$

Question 202:

Differentiate and simplify $y = x(x+3)^4$

A. $(x+3)^3$
B. $(x+3)^4$
C. $x(x+3)^3$
D. $(5x+3)(x+3)^3$
E. $5x^3(x+3)$

Question 203:

Evaluate $\int_1^2 \frac{2}{x^2} dx$

A. -1
B. $\frac{1}{3}$
C. 1
D. $\frac{21}{4}$
E. 2

Question 204:

Express $\frac{5i}{1+2i}$ in the form $a + bi$

A. $1 + 2i$
B. $4i$
C. $1 - 2i$
D. $2 + i$
E. $5 - i$

Question 205:
Simplify $7\log_a(2) - 3\log_a(12) + 5\log_a(3)$

A. $log_{2a}(18)$
B. $log_a(18)$
C. $log_a(7)$
D. $9log_a(17)$
E. $-log_a(7)$

Question 206:
What is the equation of the asymptote of the function $y = \frac{2x^2-x+3}{x^2+x-2}$

A. $x = 0$ B. $x = 2$ C. $y = 0.5$ D. $y = 0$ E. $y = 2$

Question 207:
Find the intersection(s) of the functions $y = e^x - 3$ and $y = 1 - 3e^{-x}$

A. 0 and ln(3)
B. 1
C. In(4) and 1
D. In(3)

Question 208:
Find the radius of the circle $x^2 + y^2 - 6x + 8y - 12 = 0$

A. 3 B. $\sqrt{13}$ C. 5 D. $\sqrt{37}$ E. 12

Question 209:
What value of a minimises $\int_0^a 2\sin(-x)\,dx$?

A. 0.5π B. π C. 2π D. 3π E. 4π

Question 210:
When $\frac{2x+3}{(x-2)(x-3)^2}$ is expressed as partial fractions, what is the numerator in the $\frac{A}{(x-2)}$ term:

A. -7 B. -1 C. 3 D. 6 E. 7

SECTION 2

Section 2 of the ENGAA consists of 17 MCQs normally organised into 4 groups. You have 40 minutes to answer all the questions. Section 2 requires the same core knowledge as section 1.

Watch the Clock

The key to maximising your score is to have a strategy of how best to use your time. Each question is split into four parts, but not all parts are worth the same number of marks. Firstly, you should be aware of how long you should ideally be spending on each question on average. With 32 marks available this equates to around one mark per minute, but some will take longer than others. An easier goal is to think that four questions of 6-8 marks each in 40 minutes means you should spend under 10 minutes per question to (ideally) leave time for reading and checking.

Start with the 'Low Hanging Fruit'

If you see a question you know immediately how to tackle, that is where you should start. This will give you marks in the bank, leaving extra time, and will also build your confidence like a warm up lap before tackling the more challenging or unfamiliar questions. As the grouped questions follow on from each other that might mean answering the beginning of all four questions, or one question entirely, whichever you are most comfortable with. However, be warned that the more you jump around between different types of question, the more likely you are to make mistakes or waste time reacquainting yourself with the problem at hand. Once you've gone through the paper once and answered the 'obvious' questions, you can then reassess how long you have left and how many questions remain to decide how long to give each question before moving on.

Use the Question Structure

Since each question is split into four parts, it's best to look ahead to the later parts of a question if you find yourself stuck on the earlier ones. These can sometimes help clarify what is expected of you at an earlier stage if you are unsure, will rely on information you have previously calculated and therefore give you a hint as to how to tackle an earlier part of the problem, remind you of a relevant formula or simply provide a clearer direction. Equally, there may be unrelated or extension questions that do not require the answers to previous sections and by not reading on you have missed out on those marks.

Proceed by Elimination

The biggest difference between the ENGAA and most other exams is that it is multiple choice. You can use this to your advantage to save time as a quick glance at the possible answers will give you more direction and understanding of what is expected of you and where to aim for. However, do not spend a long time reading all of the potential answers as this will distract you from actually solving the problem. Once you have progressed a certain way through a question, if it is obvious that you can eliminate options leaving only one possibility, there is no need to continue – you can answer the question so move on. You are not penalised for incorrect answers so there is no reason to leave the exam with any blanks. If you have run out of time, or a question is taking much longer than it should, make an educated guess and move on.

Practice

The best way to prepare is to practice not only long answer questions of this level, but also different multiple choice papers to familiarise yourself with how to eliminate options and get to the answer as fast as possible. As the exam is relatively new, there are not many past papers to use, however there are several exam boards as well as competitions like the Canadian Maths Competition that are multiple choice, which you can use for practice.

Thrive on Adversity

The ENGAA is specifically designed to be challenging and to take you out of your comfort zone. This is done in order to separate different tiers of students depending on their academic ability. The reason for this type of exam is that Cambridge attracts excellent students that will almost invariable score well in exams. If, for this reason, during your preparation, you come across questions that you find very difficult, use this as motivation to try and further your knowledge beyond the simple school syllabus. This is where the option for specialisation ties in.

Practice Calculus

Practicing calculus might seem unnecessary. But it will give you a big advantage to be confident with it as you will be significantly more efficient and faster. As the math part is core knowledge for all section 2 questions, you can be certain that to some degree or other you will be required to apply your calculus.

Think in Applied Formulas

Trying to answer section 2 physics questions without first learning all the core formulas is like trying to run before you can walk – ensure you're completely confident with all the core formulas before starting the practice questions.

Variety

Physics is a very varied subject, and the questions you may be asked in an exam will reflect this variety. Many students have a preferred area within physics, e.g. electronics, astrophysics or mechanics. However, it is important to remember not to neglect any subject area in its entirety. It is entirely possible that of the four main questions in the ENGAA, several of them could be outside of you comfort zone – leaving you in a very bad position.

Graphs

Graph sketching is usually a tricky area for many students. When tackling a graph sketching problem, there are many approaches however it is useful to start with the basics:

- What is the value of y when x is zero?
- What is the value of x when y is zero?
- Are there any special values of x and y?
- If there is a fraction involved, at what values of x is the numerator or denominator equal to zero?

If you asked to draw a function that is the sum, product or division of two (sub) functions, start by drawing out all of the sub functions. Which function is the dominant function when $x > 0$ and $x < 0$.
Answering these basic questions will tell you where the asymptotes and intercepts etc. are, which will help with drawing the function.

Remember the Basics

A surprisingly large number of students do not know what the properties of basic shapes etc. are. For example, the area of a circle is πr^2, the surface area of a sphere is $4\pi r^2$ and the volume of a sphere is $\frac{4}{3}\pi r^3$. To 'go up' a dimension (i.e. to go from an area to a volume) you need to integrate and to 'go down' a dimension you need to differentiate. Learning this will make it easy to remember formulas for the areas and volumes of basic shapes.

It is also important to remember important formulas even though they may be included in formula booklets. The reason for this is that although you may have access to formula booklets during exams, this will not be the case in interviews which will follow the NSAA. In addition, flicking through formula booklets takes up time during an exam and can be avoided if you are able to memorise important formulas.

SECTION 2 Questions

Question 1.1
A golfer swings a club so that the head completes a (virtually) complete circle in T=0.1 s. The length of the club is R=1 m.

What angle from the horizontal should the club hit the ball at to maximise the distance travelled?

[1 mark]

A. 0°
B. 30°
C. 45°
D. 90°
E. Any angle

Question 1.2
What is the (approximate) velocity of the club when it strikes the ball?

[1 mark]

A. 0.1 m/s
B. 3 m/s
C. 10 m/s
D. 60 m/s
E. 100 m/s

Question 1.3
Assuming that the ground is flat, what is the total time the golf ball is in the air?

[3 marks]

A. $3\sqrt{2}$ s
B. $5\sqrt{2}$ s
C. $6\sqrt{2}$ s
D. 12 s
E. 15 s

Question 1.4
What therefore is the maximum horizontal distance the ball travels?

[2 marks]

A. 180 m
B. $180\sqrt{2}$ m
C. 360 m
D. $360\sqrt{2}$ m
E. 720 m

Question 2.1

What is the mass of the moon in terms of the radius of the earth, r, if the density of the Moon is 75% of the density of earth, ρ, and that the radius of the Moon is 4 times smaller than the radius of Earth.

[1 mark]

A. $\frac{1}{64}\rho\pi r^3$

B. $\frac{9}{16}\rho\pi r^3$

C. $\frac{3}{64}\rho\pi r^2$

D. $\frac{3}{64}\rho\pi r^3$

E. $\frac{1}{16}\rho\pi r^3$

Question 2.2

Given that gravitational force is determined by $F = G\frac{Mm}{R^2}$, which of the following is an expression for the acceleration due to gravity on earth, where G is the gravitational constant?

[1 mark]

A. $G\rho\pi r^2$

B. $\frac{3}{4}G\rho\pi r$

C. $\frac{4}{3}G\rho\pi r^2$

D. $\frac{1}{16}G\rho\pi r$

E. $\frac{4}{3}G\rho\pi r$

Question 2.3

Estimate the gravitational acceleration at the surface of the Moon relative to g on earth.

[3 marks]

A. $8g$

B. $\frac{g}{8}$

C. $\frac{g}{16}$

D. $\frac{3g}{16}$

E. $\frac{7g}{16}$

Question 2.4

How would the orbital speed of a satellite of equal mass and equal orbital radius change between orbiting earth and the moon?

[2 marks]

A. Decrease by a factor of $\sqrt{3}/4$

B. Decrease by a factor of $\frac{7}{16}$

C. It will be remain unchanged

D. Increase by a factor of $\frac{1}{16}$

E. Increase by a factor of 8

Question 3.1

Identical resistors are connected using wire of negligible resistance to a 1.4 V power supply. What would the resistance be of two resistors in parallel?

[1 mark]

A. 2R B. $\frac{R}{2}$ C. $\frac{3R}{2}$ D. $\frac{2R}{3}$ E. R

Question 3.2

What would the total resistance in this circuit be, considering all the resistors to be identical?

[4 marks]

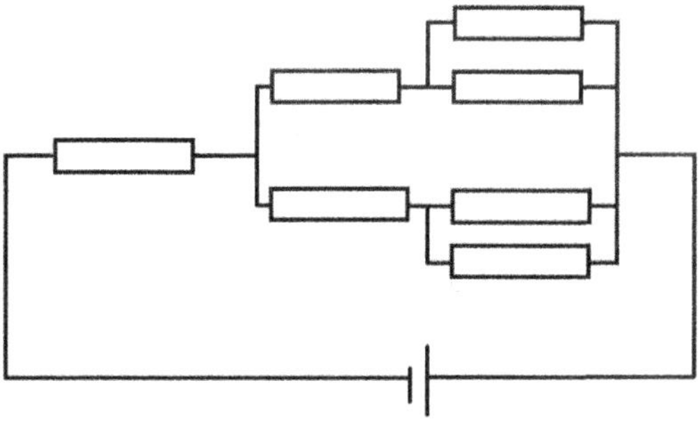

A. 7R

B. 3R

C. $\frac{7R}{3}$

D. $\frac{3R}{4}$

E. $\frac{7R}{4}$

Question 3.3
What would R be to produce a total current of 2 A?

[1 mark]

A. 0.01 Ω
B. 0.4 Ω
C. 0.2 Ω
D. 0.5 Ω
E. 1 Ω

Question 3.4
What would be the power dissipated in the circuit?

[1 mark]

A. 0.6 W
B. 1.2 W
C. 2.3 W
D. 2.8 W
E. 3.2 W

Question 4.1: The position of a particle the moves along the x axis is given by the equation $x = 10 + 1.5t^3$. What expression would represent the velocity of the particle?

A. $v = 1 + 1.5t^2$
B. $v = 4.5t^2$
C. $v = 10 + 4.5t^2$
D. $v = 45 + 4.5t^3$
E. $v = 3.0t^3$

Question 4.2: For what time t the acceleration of the particle is equal to zero?

A. $t = 20\ s$
B. $t = 10\ s$
C. $t = 4.5\ s$
D. $t = 0$
E. $t = 1.5\ s$

Question 4.3: What would the average velocity and of the particle approximately be for the interval for t = 2s to t=10s

A. $v = 150\ m/s$
B. $v = 400\ m/s$
C. $v = 190\ m/s$
D. $v = 250\ m/s$
E. $v = 3.0t^3$

Question 4.4: If the equation represents the motion of the ball of mass m that is thrown against a wall located away from the initial location of the ball, what will be the energy transferred to the wall in an elastic collision considering that the ball travels for 5 seconds until it hits the wall.

A. $E = 780m\ J$
B. $E = 500m\ J$
C. $E = 1300m\ J$

Question 5.1

A lift with a mass of 800 kg can carry up to 700 kg of passengers. Calculate the total energy needed for an electric motor is used to raise the elevator with a full load from the ground floor to the third floor, 7 m higher. [assume $g=10\ m/s^2$]

[1 mark]

A. 105 J
B. 210 J
C. 105 kJ
D. 210 kJ
E. 105 MJ

Question 5.2

Calculate the power of motor required to do this in 30 s.

[1 mark]

A. 700 W
B. 3500 W
C. 7 kW
D. 35 kW
E. 70 kW

Question 5.3

Find the average kinetic energy of the lift and passengers during the ascent.

[2 marks]

A. 41 J
B. 52 J
C. 67 J
D. 82 J
E. 105 J

Question 5.4

The elevator takes 10 s to accelerate and 10 s to decelerate using the same magnitude of constant force in each case. Between acceleration and deceleration no force is used. Calculate the greatest speed which the lift attains.

[3 marks]

A. 0.04 ms^{-1}
B. 0.14 ms^{-1}
C. 0.35 ms^{-1}
D. 1.3 ms^{-1}
E. 2.3 ms^{-1}

Question 6.1

If the friction coefficient between m_1 and m_2 is μ_1 and between m_2 and the inclined plane is μ_2, (where α = the angle of inclination) determine the acceleration of m_2.

[2 marks]

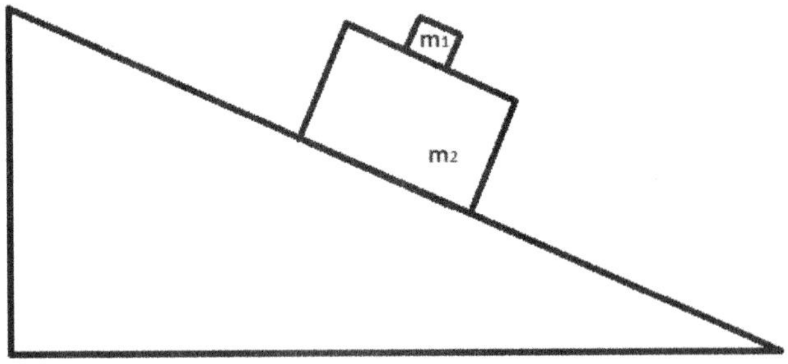

A. $g(1 - \mu_2 \cos\alpha)$
B. $g(\mu_2 \sin\alpha - \mu_1 \cos\alpha)$
C. $mg(\sin\alpha - \mu_2 \cos\alpha)$
D. $g(\sin\alpha - \mu_1 \cos\alpha)$
E. $g(\sin\alpha - \mu_2 \cos\alpha)$

Question 6.2

Determine the acceleration of m_1 with respect to the plane

[2 marks]

A. $g(\sin\alpha - \mu_1\cos\alpha)$
B. $mg(\sin\alpha - \mu_1\cos\alpha)$
C. $g\sin\alpha(\mu_1 - \mu_2)$
D. $g(\sin\alpha - \cos\alpha)$
E. $g(\mu_2\sin\alpha - \mu_1\cos\alpha)$

Question 6.3

Determine the acceleration of m_1 with respect to m_2

[2 marks]

A. $g\cos\alpha(\mu_1 + \mu_2)$
B. $g\cos\alpha(\mu_2 - \mu_1)$
C. $g\sin\alpha(\mu_1 - \mu_2)$
D. $mg\cos\alpha(\mu_1 - \mu_2)$
E. $mg\cos\alpha(\mu_1 + \mu_2)$

Question 6.4

Which of the following would give the coefficient of friction?

[1 mark]

A. $\tan(\alpha)$
B. $\cos(\alpha)$
C. $\sin(\alpha)$
D. mg
E. $mg\tan(\alpha)$

Question 7.1: The graph below represents the velocity as a function of time of a car (mass of 1000 kg) moving in a stray line. How far has the car travelled after 30 min?

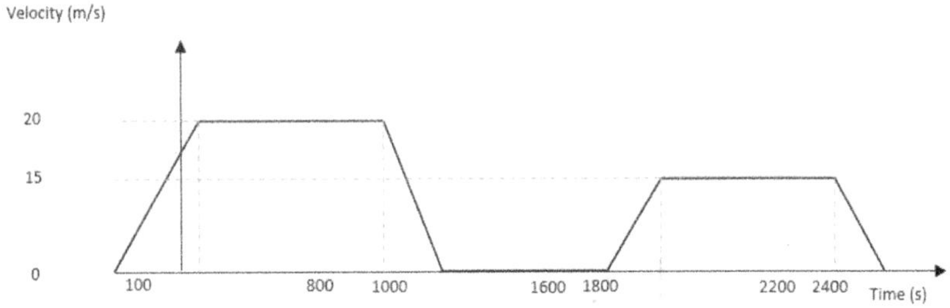

A. $4900\ m$
B. $9000\ m$
C. $2000\ m$
D. $5000\ m$
E. $5900\ m$

Question 7.2: Compute the following calculation $\int_{1600}^{1800} v\, dt$. Select the option that represents the correct corresponding value and its physical meaning.

A. $1500\ m$; acceleration
B. $2300\ m$; acceleration
C. $1500\ m$; velocity
D. $2000\ m$, distance
E. $1500\ m$, distance

Question 7.3: Calculate the force exerted on the car at t = 900s would be?

A. $110\ N$
B. $100\ N$
C. $75\ N$
D. $500\ N$
E. $765\ N$

Question 7.4: What is the power delivered by the car's engine in the interval of 0 – 100 s?

A. 2 kW
B. 900 W
C. 1.5 kW
D. 2.5 kW
E. 1.05 kW

Question 8.1: The following diagram represents the horizontal component of a force acting over a particle. If the particle is at rest at x = 0, what is its position (along the x-axis) when its velocity is maximum?

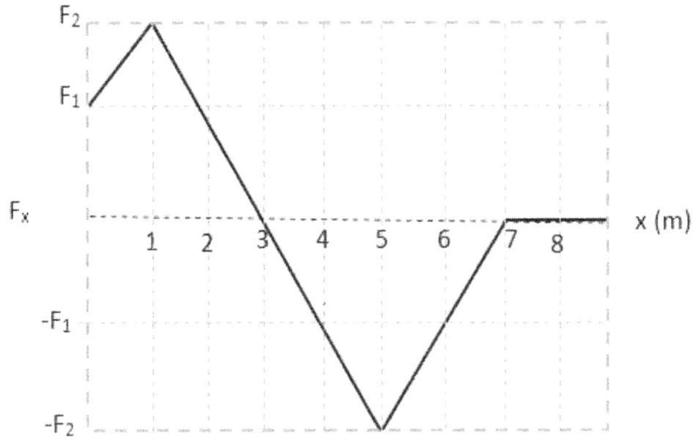

A. 1 m
B. 5 m
C. 3 m
D. 4 m
E. 8 m

Question 8.2: What is the particle position (along the x-axis) when its kinetic energy is maximum?

A. $1\,m$
B. $5\,m$
C. $7\,m$
D. $3\,m$
E. $8\,m$

Question 8.3: What is the particle position (along the x-axis) when its velocity is zero?

A. $6\,m$
B. $1\,m$
C. $7\,m$
D. $3\,m$
E. $8\,m$

Question 8.4: After x = 6m, is correct to say about the particle:

A. The velocity vector is pointing in the same sense as it is in x=3m
B. The velocity vector is equal to zero
C. The acceleration vector is pointing in the same sense as it is in x=2m
D. The acceleration vector is point in the opposite sense as it is in x =2m

Question 9.1: A little girl throws vertically a ball (m=0.5 kg) in the air, at t =0. What of the following graphs would better describe the velocity of the ball as a function of time? Disregard the influence of air in the movement of the ball. The y axis is velocity and the x axis is time.

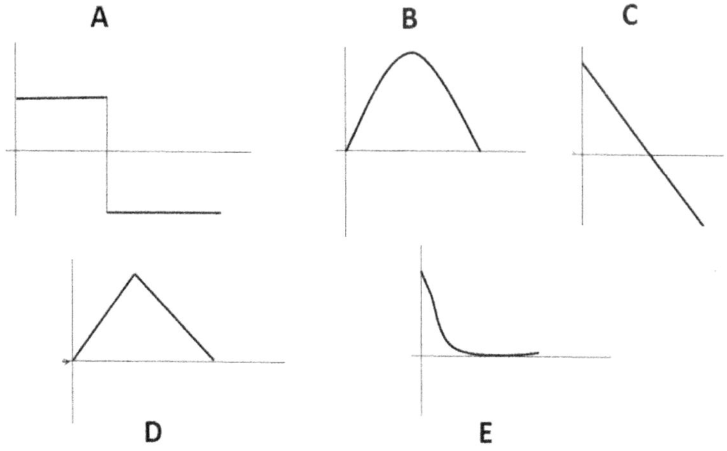

Question 9.2: If the ball leaves the girl's hand at 15 m/s what approximately is the highest point from the ground the ball can reach? Disregard the influence of air.

A. $6\ m$ B. $12\ m$ C. $25\ m$ D. $3.5\ m$ E. $8\ m$

Question 9.3: Approximately, how long does the ball take to reach the highest point of its trajectory?

A. $1.5\ s$ B. $10\ s$ C. $5\ s$ D. $4\ s$ E. $9.5\ s$

Question 9.4: What would the potential and Kinetic energy of the ball be, respectively, 5.0m from the ground?

A. $31.75\,J\ and\ 24.5\,J$
B. $25.5\,J\ and\ 37.75\,J$
C. $24.5\,J\ and\ 31.75\,J$
D. $30\,J\ and\ 26\,J$
E. $11\,J\ and\ 27\,J$

Question 10.1: A horizontal force is applied to the ramp (object 1) (m=10kg) as shown in the figure. There is no friction between the ramp and the ground and the coefficient of friction between the ramp and object 2 (m=10kg), is $\mu = 0.2$. What option correctly demonstrates the forces applied over object 2?

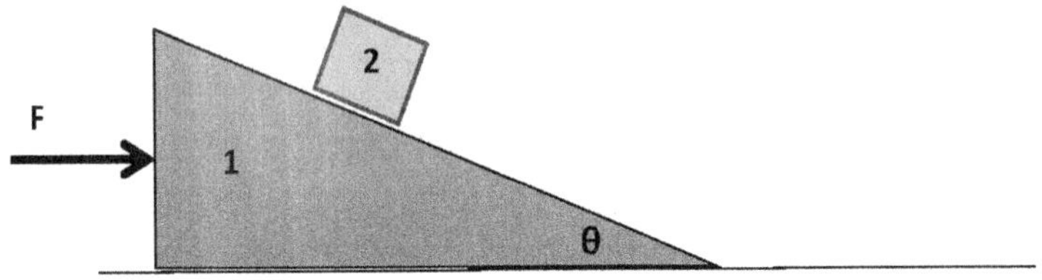

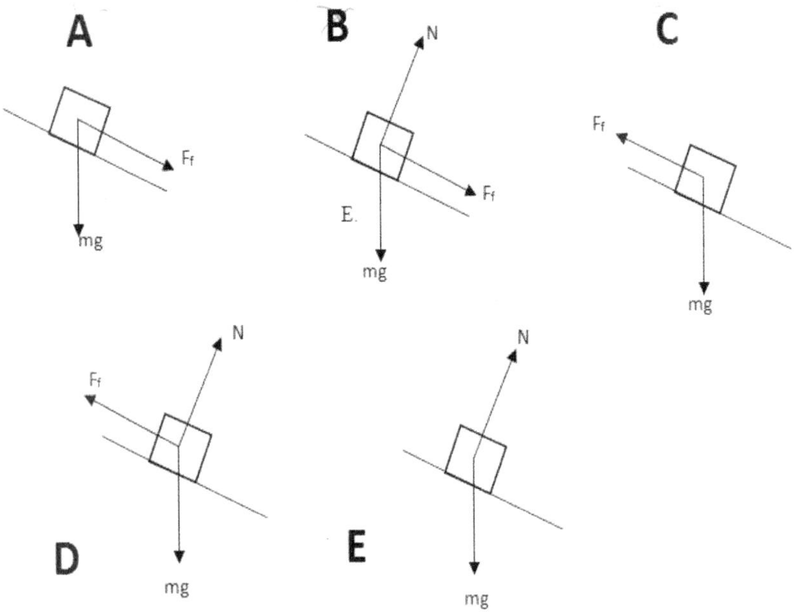

Question 10.2: Express the weight of object 2 as a function of the angle θ and the coefficient of friction μ.

A. $mg = N\mu(sin\theta - cos\theta)$
B. $mg = N\mu(cos\theta + sin\theta)$
C. $mg = N(\mu sin\theta - cos\theta)$
D. $mg = \mu(sin\theta + Ncos\theta)$
E. $mg = N(cos\theta - \mu sin\theta)$

Question 10.3: Express the acceleration of object 2, in relation to the object 1, as a function of the angle θ and the coefficient of friction μ.

A. $a = N(sin\theta - \mu cos\theta)$
B. $a = \frac{N}{m_2}(sin\theta - \mu cos\theta)$
C. $a = \frac{N}{m_2}(cos\theta + \mu cos\theta)$
D. $a = \frac{N}{m_2}(sin\theta + \mu cos\theta)$
E. $a = \frac{N}{m_2}(cos\theta + \mu sin\theta)$

Question 10.4: What is the maximum value of the force F, in Newtons, that can be applied without provoking the movement of object 2 upwards along the ramp? Consider $sin\theta = 0.6\ and\ cos\theta = 0.8$

A. $219\ N$ B. $350\ N$ C. $200N$ D. $155\ N$ E. $149\ N$

ANSWERS

Answer Key

Q	A	Q	A	Q	A	Q	A	Q	A	Q	A	Q	A
1	F	31	C	61	D	91	A	121	B	151	D	181	C
2	A	32	G	62	F	92	D	122	A	152	D	182	C
3	D	33	D	63	B	93	A	123	F	153	B	183	E
4	E	34	D	64	A	94	B	124	D	154	E	184	C
5	G	35	E	65	C	95	C	125	A	155	E	185	C
6	C	36	B	66	C	96	D	126	B	156	B	186	A
7	D	37	A	67	G	97	A	127	A	157	C	187	D
8	E	38	E	68	C	98	B	128	F	158	A	188	C
9	D	39	D	69	B	99	C	129	D	159	C	189	B
10	D	40	F	70	B	100	E	130	A	160	B	190	A
11	F	41	E	71	E	101	B	131	D	161	B	191	C
12	B	42	A	72	C	102	C	132	D	162	B	192	C
13	C	43	B	73	E	103	C	133	F	163	C	193	E
14	G	44	C	74	E	104	C	134	B	164	C	194	E
15	D	45	D	75	D	105	E	135	C	165	A	195	A
16	E	46	F	76	E	106	A	136	B	166	C	196	C
17	A	47	E	77	E	107	C	137	C	167	D	197	C
18	E	48	C	78	C	108	E	138	A	168	C	198	E
19	G	49	C	79	E	109	E	139	A	169	D	199	A
20	E	50	B	80	D	110	C	140	C	170	A	200	D
21	H	51	D	81	A	111	E	141	B	171	C	201	C
22	E	52	F	82	B	112	E	142	D	172	B	202	D
23	G	53	G	83	C	113	E	143	C	173	B	203	A
24	D	54	D	84	D	114	B	144	A	174	A	204	D
25	E	55	D	85	B	115	C	145	C	175	C	205	B
26	D	56	A	86	D	116	B	146	C	176	C	206	E
27	G	57	E	87	C	117	B	147	C	177	B	207	A
28	F	58	C	88	E	118	C	148	B	178	A	208	D
29	B	59	D	89	C	119	D	149	D	179	C	209	C
30	A	60	C	90	A	120	C	150	E	180	E	210	E

Section 1: Worked Answers

Question 1: F

That the amplitude of a wave determines its mass is false. Waves are not objects and do not have mass.

Question 2: A

We know that displacement s = 30 m, initial speed u = 0 ms^{-1}, acceleration a = 5.4 ms^{-2}, final speed v = ? time t = ?

And that $v^2 = u^2 + 2as$

$v^2 = 0 + 2 \times 5.4 \times 30$

$v^2 = 324$ so v = 18 ms^{-1}

and $s = ut + 1/2\ at^2$ so $30 = 1/2 \times 5.4 \times t^2$

$t^2 = 30/2.7$ so t = 3.3 s

Question 3: D

The wavelength is given by: velocity v = λf and frequency f = 1/T so v = λ/T giving wavelength λ = vT

The period T = 49 s/7 so λ = 5 ms^{-1} x 7 s = 35 m

Question 4: E

This is a straightforward question as you only have to put the numbers into the equation (made harder by the numbers being hard to work with).

$$Power = \frac{Force\ x\ Distance}{Time} = \frac{375\ N\ x\ 1.3\ m}{5\ s}$$

$$= 75\ x\ 1.3 = 97.5\ W$$

Question 5: G

v = u + at

v = 0 + 5.6 x 8 = 44.8 ms^{-1}

And $s = ut + \frac{at^2}{2} = 0 + 5.6 \text{ x} \frac{8^2}{2} = 179.2$

Question 6: C

The sky diver leaves the plane and will accelerate until the air resistance equals their weight – this is their terminal velocity. The sky diver will accelerate under the force of gravity. If the air resistance force exceeded the force of gravity the sky diver would accelerate away from the ground, and if it was less than the force of gravity they would continue to accelerate toward the ground.

Question 7: D

$s = 20$ m, $u = 0$ ms^{-1}, $a = 10$ ms^{-2}

and $v^2 = u^2 + 2as$

$v^2 = 0 + 2 \times 10 \times 20$

$v^2 = 400$; $v = 20$ ms^{-1}

Momentum = Mass x velocity = 20 x 0.1 = 2 kgms^{-1}

Question 8: E

Electromagnetic waves have varying wavelengths and frequencies and their energy is proportional to their frequency.

Question 9: D

The total resistance = R + r = 0.8 + 1 = 1.8 Ω

and $I = \frac{e.m.f}{total\ resistance} = \frac{36}{1.8} = 20\ A$

Question 10: D

Use Newton's second law and remember to work in SI units:

So $Force = mass \times accelaration = mass \times \frac{\Delta velocity}{time}$

$$= 20 \times 10^{-3} \times \frac{100 - 0}{10 \times 10^{-3}}$$

$= 200\ N$

Question 11: F

In this case, the work being done is moving the bag 0.7 m

i.e. $Work\ Done\ =\ Bag's\ Weight\ x\ Distance\ =\ 50 \text{ x } 10 \text{ x } 0.7 = 350\ N$

$Power = \frac{Work}{Time} = \frac{350}{3} = 116.7 \text{ W}$

= 117 W to 3 significant figures

Question 12: B

Firstly, use P = Fv to calculate the power [Ignore the frictional force as we are not concerned with the resultant force here].

So P = 300 x 30 = 9000 W

Then, use P = IV to calculate the current.

I = P/V = 9000/200 = 45 A

Question 13: C

Work is defined as W = F x s. Work can also be defined as work = force x distance moved in the direction of force. Work is measured in joules and 1 Joule = 1 Newton x 1 Metre, and 1 Newton = 1 Kg x ms^{-2} [F = ma].

Thus, 1 Joule = Kgm^2s^{-2}

Question 14: G

Joules are the unit of energy (and also Work = Force x Distance). Thus, 1 Joule = 1 N x 1 m.

Pa is the unit of Pressure (= Force/Area). Thus, Pa = N x m^{-2}. So J = Nm^{-2} x m^3 = Pa x m^3. Newton's third law describes that every action produces an equal and opposite reaction. For this reason, the energy required to decelerate a body is equal to the amount of energy it possess during movement, i.e. its kinetic energy, which is defined as in statement 1.

Question 15: D

Alpha radiation is of the lower energy, as it represents the movement of a fairly large particle consisting of 2 neutrons and 2 protons. Beta radiation consists of high-energy, high-speed electrons or positrons.

Question 16: E

The half-life does depend on atom type and isotope, as these parameters significantly impact on the physical properties of the atom in general, so statement 1 is false. Statement 2 is the correct definition of half-life. Statement 3 is also correct: half-life in exponential decay will always have the same duration, independent of the quantity of the matter in question; in non-exponential decay, half-life is dependent on the quantity of matter in question.

Question 17: A

In contrast to nuclear fission, where neutrons are shot at unstable atoms, nuclear fusion is based on the high speed, high-temperature collision of molecules, most commonly hydrogen, to form a new, stable atom while releasing energy.

Question 18: E

Nuclear fission releases a significant amount of energy, which is the basis of many nuclear weapons. Shooting neutrons at unstable atoms destabilises the nuclei which in turn leads to a chain reaction and fission. Nuclear fission can lead to the release of ionizing gamma radiation.

Question 19: G

The total resistance of the circuit would be twice the resistance of one resistor and proportional to the voltage, as given by Ohm's Law. Since it is a series circuit, the same current flows through each resistor and since they are identical the potential difference across each resistor will be the same.

Question 20: E

The distance between Earth and Sun = Time x Speed = 60×8 seconds $\times 3 \times 10^8\ ms^{-1} = 480 \times 3 \times 10^8$ m

Approximately = $1500 \times 10^8 = 1.5 \times 10^{11}$ m.

The circumference of Earth's orbit around the sun is given by $2\pi r = 2 \times 3 \times 1.5 \times 10^{11}$

$= 9 \times 10^{11} = 10^{12}$ m

Question 21: H

Speed is a scalar quantity whilst velocity is a vector describing both magnitude and direction. Speed describes the distance a moving object covers over time (i.e. speed = distance/time), whereas velocity describes the rate of change of the displacement of an object (i.e. velocity = displacement/time). The internationally standardised unit for speed is meters per second (ms^{-1}), while ms^{-2} is the unit of acceleration.

Question 22: E

Ohm's Law only applies to conductors and can be mathematically expressed as $V \alpha I$. The easiest way to do this is to write down the equations for statements c, d and e. C: $I \alpha \frac{1}{V}$; D: $I \alpha V^2$; E: $I \alpha V$. Thus, statement E is correct.

Question 23: G

Any object at rest is not accelerating and therefore has no resultant force. Strictly speaking, Newton's second law is actually: Force = rate of change of momentum, which can be manipulated to give statement 2:

$$Force = \frac{momentum}{time} = \frac{mass \text{ x } velocity}{time} = mass \text{ x } accelaration$$

Question 24: D

Statement 3 is incorrect, as $Charge = Current\ x\ time$. Statement 1 substitutes $I = \frac{V}{R}$ and statement 2 substitutes $I = \frac{P}{V}$.

Question 25: E

Weight of elevator + people = mg = 10 x (1600 + 200) = 18,000 N

Applying Newton's second law of motion on the car gives:

Thus, the resultant force is given by:

F_M = Motor Force – [Frictional Force + Weight]

F_M = M – 4,000 – 18,000

Use Newton's second law to give: F_M = M – 22,000 N = ma

Thus, M – 22,000 N = 1,800a

Since the lift must accelerate at $1ms^{-2}$: M = 1,800 kg x 1 ms^{-2} + 22,000 N

M = 23,800 N

Question 26: D

Total Distance = Distance during acceleration phase + Distance during braking phase

Distance during acceleration phase is given by:

$$s = ut + \frac{at^2}{2} = 0 + \frac{5 \text{ x } 10^2}{2} = 250\,m$$

$v = u + at = 0 + 5\,x\,10 = 50\,ms^{-1}$

And use $a = \frac{v-u}{t}$ to calculate the deceleration: $a = \frac{0-50}{20} = -2.5 \text{ ms}^{-2}$

Distance during the deceleration phase is given by:

$$s = ut + \frac{at^2}{2} = 50\,x\,20 + \frac{-2.5 \text{ x } 20^2}{2} = 1000 - \frac{2.5 \text{ x } 400}{2}$$

$s = 1000 - 500 = 500\,m$

Thus, $Total\ Distance = 250 + 500 = 750\,m$

Question 27: G

It is not possible to calculate the power of the heater as we don't know the current that flows through it or its internal resistance. The 8 ohms refers to the external copper wire and not the heater. Whilst it's important that you know how to use equations like P = IV, it's more important that you know when you ***can't*** use them!

Question 28: F

This question has a lot of numbers but not any information on time, which is necessary to calculate power. You cannot calculate power by using P= IV as you don't know how many electrons are accelerated through the potential difference per unit time. Thus, more information is required to calculate the power.

Question 29: B

When an object is in equilibrium with its surroundings, it radiates and absorbs energy at the same rate and so its temperature remains constant i.e. there is no *net* energy transfer. Radiation is slower than conduction and convection.

Question 30: A

The work done by the force is given by: $Work\ Done = Force \times Distance = 12\ N \times 3\ m = 36\ J$

Since the surface is frictionless, $Work\ Done = Kinetic\ Energy$.

$E_k = \frac{mv^2}{2} = \frac{6v^2}{2}$

Thus, $36 = 3v^2$

$v = \sqrt{12} = \sqrt{4}\sqrt{3} = 2\sqrt{3}\ ms^{-1}$

Question 31: C

$Total\ energy\ supplied\ to\ water$
$= Change\ in\ temperature \times Mass\ of\ water \times 4{,}000\ J$
$= 40 \times 1.5 \times 4{,}000 = 240{,}000\ J$

$Power\ of\ the\ heater = \frac{Work\ Done}{time} = \frac{240{,}000}{50 \times 60} = \frac{240{,}000}{3{,}000} = 80\ W$

Using $P = IV = \frac{V^2}{R}$:

$R = \frac{V^2}{P} = \frac{100^2}{80} = \frac{10{,}000}{80} = 125\ ohms$

Question 32: G

The large amount of energy released during atomic fission is the basis underlying nuclear power plants. Splitting an atom into two or more parts will by definition produce molecules of different sizes than the original atom; therefore it produces two new atoms. The free neutrons and photons produced by the splitting of atoms form the basis of the energy release.

Question 33: D

Gravitational potential energy is just an extension of the equation work done = force x distance (force is the weight of the object, *mg*, and distance is the height, *h*). The reservoir in statement 3 would have a potential energy of 10^{10} Joules i.e. 10 Giga Joules ($E_p = 10^6$ kg x 10 N x 10^3 m).

Question 34: D

Statement 1 is the common formulation of Newton's third law. Statement 2 presents a consequence of the application of Newton's third law.

Statement 3 is false: rockets can still accelerate because the products of burning fuel are ejected in the opposite direction from which the rocket needs to accelerate.

Question 35: E

Positively charged objects have lost electrons.

$Charge = Current \times Time = \frac{Voltage}{Resistance} \times Time.$

Objects can become charged by friction as electrons are transferred from one object to the other.

Question 36: B

Each body of mass exerts a gravitational force on another body with mass. This is true for all planets as well.

Gravitational force is dependent on the mass of both objects. Satellites stay in orbit due to centripetal force that acts tangentially to gravity (not because of the thrust from their engines). Two objects will only land at the same time if they also have the same shape or they are in a vaccum (as otherwise air resistance would result in different terminal velocities).

Question 37: A

Metals conduct electrical charge easily and provide little resistance to the flow of electrons. Charge can also flow in several directions. However, all conductors have an internal resistance and therefore provide *some* resistance to electrical charge.

Question 38: E

First, calculate the rate of petrol consumption:

$$\frac{Speed}{Consumption} = \frac{60\ miles/hour}{30\ miles/gallon} = 2\ gallons/hour$$

Therefore, the total power is:

$$2\ gallons\ =\ 2\ x\ 9\ x\ 10^8 = 18\ x\ 10^8 J$$

$$1\ hour\ =\ 60\ x\ 60\ =\ 3600\ s$$

$$\text{Power} = \frac{Energy}{Time} = \frac{18\ x 10^8}{3600}$$

$$\text{P}= \frac{18}{36} \text{ x } 10^6 = 5 \text{ x } 10^5\ W$$

Since efficiency is 20%, the power delivered to the wheels = $5 \text{ x } 10^5 \text{ x } 0.2 = 10^5\ W = 100\ kW$

Question 39: D

Beta radiation is stopped by a few millimetres of aluminium, but not by paper. In β^- radiation, a neutron changes into a proton plus an emitted electron. This means the atomic mass number remains unchanged.

Question 40: F

Firstly, calculate the mass of the car = $\frac{Weight}{g} = \frac{15{,}000}{10} = 1{,}500\ kg$

Then using $v = u + at$ where v = 0 ms^{-1} and u = 15 ms^{-1} and t = 10 x 10^{-3} s

$$a = \frac{0-15}{0.01} = 1500 ms^{-2}$$

$$F = ma = 1500\ x\ 1500 = 2\ 250\ 000\ N$$

Question 41: E

Electrical insulators offer high resistance to the flow of charge. Insulators are usually non-metals; metals conduct charge very easily. Since charge does not flow easily to even out, they can be charged with friction.

Question 42: A

The car accelerates for the first 10 seconds at a constant rate and then decelerates after t=30 seconds. It does not reverse, as the velocity is not negative. Therefore only statement 1 is not true.

Question 43: B

The distance travelled by the car is represented by the area under the curve (integral of velocity) which is given by the area of two triangles and a rectangle:

$$Area = \left(\frac{1}{2}\ x\ 10\ x\ 10\right) + (20\ x\ 10) + \left(\frac{1}{2}\ x\ 10\ x\ 10\right)$$

$$Area = 50 + 200 + 50 = 300\ m$$

Question 44: C

Using the equation force = mass x acceleration, where the unknown acceleration = change in velocity over change in time.

Hence: $\frac{F}{m} = \frac{change\ in\ velocity}{change\ in\ time}$

We know that F = 10,000 N, mass = 1,000 kg and change in time is 5 seconds.

So, $\frac{10{,}000}{1{,}000} = \frac{change\ in\ velocity}{5}$

So change in velocity $= 10 \text{ x } 5 = 50\ m/s$

Question 45: D

This question tests both your ability to convert unusual units into SI units and to select the relevant values (e.g. the crane's mass is not important here).

0.01 tonnes = 10 kg; 100 cm = 1 m; 5,000 ms = 5 s

$$Power = \frac{Work\ Done}{Time} = \frac{Force \text{ x } Distance}{Time}$$

In this case the force is the weight of the wardrobe $= 10 \text{ x } g = 10 \text{ x } 10 = 100N$

Thus, $Power = \frac{100 \text{ x } 1}{5} = 20\ W$

Question 46: F

Remember that the resistance of a parallel circuit (R_T) is given by: $\frac{1}{R_T} = \frac{1}{R_1} + \frac{1}{R_2} + \ldots$

Thus, $\frac{1}{R_T} = \frac{1}{1} + \frac{1}{2} = \frac{3}{2}$ and therefore $R = \frac{2}{3}\ \Omega$

Using Ohm's Law: $I = \frac{20\ V}{\frac{2}{3}\Omega} = 20 \text{ x } \frac{3}{2} = 30$ A

Question 47: E

Water is denser than air. Therefore, the speed of light decreases when it enters water and increases when it leaves water. The direction of light also changes when light enters/leaves water. This phenomenon is known as refraction and is governed by Snell's Law.

Question 48: C

The voltage in a parallel circuit is the same across each branch, i.e. branch *A* Voltage = branch *B* Voltage.

The resistance of Branch *A* = 6 x 5 = 30 Ω; the resistance of Branch *B* = 10 x 2 = 20 Ω.

Using Ohm's Law: I= V/R. Thus, $I_A = \frac{60}{30} = 2\ A;\ I_B = \frac{60}{20} = 3\ A$

Question 49: C

This is a very straightforward question made harder by the awkward units you have to work with. Ensure you are able to work comfortably with prefixes of 10^9 and 10^{-9} and convert without difficulty.

50,000,000,000 nano Watts = 50 W and 0.000000004 Giga Amperes = 4 A.

Using $P = IV$: $V = \frac{P}{I} = \frac{50}{4} = 12.5\ V = 0.0125\ kV$

Question 50: B

Radioactive decay is highly random and unpredictable. Only gamma decay releases gamma rays and few types of decay release X-rays. The electrical charge of an atom's nucleus decreases after alpha decay as two protons are lost.

Question 51: D

Using $P = IV$: $I = \frac{P}{V} = \frac{60}{15} = 4\,A$

Now using Ohm's Law: $R = \frac{V}{I} = \frac{15}{4} = 3.75\,\Omega$

So each resistor has a resistance of $\frac{3.75}{3} = 1.25\,\Omega$.

If two more resistors are added, the overall resistance = $1.25 \times 5 = 6.25\,\Omega$

Question 52: F

To calculate the useful work done and hence the efficiency, we must know the resistive forces on the tractor, whether it is stationery or moving at the end point and if there is any change in vertical height.

Question 53: G

Electromagnetic induction is defined by statements 1 and 2. An electrical current is generated when a coil moves in a magnetic field.

Question 54: D

An ammeter will always give the same reading in a series circuit, not in a parallel circuit where current splits at each branch in accordance with Ohm's Law.

Question 55: D

Electrons move in the opposite direction to current (i.e. they move from negative to positive).

Question 56: A

For a fixed resistor, the current is directly proportional to the potential difference. For a filament lamp, as current increases, the metal filament becomes hotter. This causes the metal atoms to vibrate and move more, resulting in more collisions with the flow of electrons. This makes it harder for the electrons to move through the lamp and results in increased resistance. Therefore, the graph's gradient decreases as current increases.

Question 57: E

Vector quantities consist of both direction and magnitude, e.g. velocity, displacement, etc., and can be added by taking account of direction in the sum.

Question 58: C

The gravity on the moon is 6 times less than 10 ms^{-2}. Thus, $g_{moon} = \frac{10}{6} = \frac{5}{3}$ ms^{-2}.

Since weight = mass x gravity, the mass of the rock = $\frac{250}{\frac{5}{3}} = \frac{750}{5} = 150\ kg$

Therefore, the density $= \frac{mass}{volume} = \frac{150}{250} = 0.6\ kg/cm^3$

Question 59: D

An alpha particle consists of a helium nucleus. Thus, alpha decay causes the mass number to decrease by 4 and the atomic number to decrease by 2. Five iterations of this would decrease the mass number by 20 and the atomic number by 10.

Question 60: C

Using Ohm's Law: The potential difference entering the transformer (V_1) = 10 x 20 = 200 V

Now use $\frac{N1}{N2} = \frac{V1}{V2}$ to give: $\frac{5}{10} = \frac{200}{V2}$

Thus, $V_2 = \frac{2,000}{5} = 400$ V

Question 61: D

For objects in free fall that have reached terminal velocity, acceleration = 0. Thus, the sphere's weight = resistive forces.

Using Work Done = Force x Distance: Force = 10,000 J/100 m = 100 N.

Therefore, the sphere's weight = 100 N and since $g = 10ms^{-2}$, the sphere's mass = 10 kg

Question 62: F

The wave length of ultraviolet waves is longer than that of x-rays. Wavelength is inversely proportional to frequency. Most electromagnetic waves are not stopped with aluminium (and require thick lead to stop them), and they travel at the speed of light. Humans can only see a very small part of the spectrum.

Question 63: B

If an object moves towards the sensor, the wavelength will appear to decrease and the frequency increase. The faster this happens, the faster the increase in frequency and decrease in wavelength.

Question 64: A

$$Acceleration = \frac{Change\ in\ Velocity}{Time} = \frac{1{,}000}{0.1} = 10{,}000\ ms^{-2}$$

Using Newton's second law: The Braking Force = Mass x Acceleration.

Thus, Braking Force = $10{,}000 \times 0.005 = 50\ N$

Question 65: C

Polonium has undergone alpha decay. Thus, Y is a helium nucleus and contains 2 protons and 2 neutrons.

Therefore, 10 moles of Y contain $2 \times 10 \times 6 \times 10^{23}$ protons = 120×10^{23} = 1.2×10^{25} protons.

Question 66: C

The rod's activity is less than 1,000 Bq after 300 days. In order to calculate the longest possible half-life, we must assume that the activity is just below 1,000 Bq after 300 days. Thus, the half-life has decreased activity from 16,0 00 Bq to 1,000 Bq in 300 days.

After one half-life: Activity = 8,000 Bq

After two half-lives: Activity = 4,000 Bq

After three half-lives: Activity = 2,000 Bq

After four half-lives: Activity = 1,000 Bq

Thus, the rod has halved its activity a minimum of 4 times in 300 days. 300/4 = 75 days

Question 67: G

There is no change in the atomic mass or proton numbers in gamma radiation. In β decay, a neutron is transformed into a proton (and an electron is released). This results in an increase in proton number by 1 but no overall change in atomic mass. Thus, after 5 rounds of beta decay, the proton number will be 89 + 5 = 94 and the mass number will remain at 200. Therefore, there are 94 protons and 200-94 = 106 neutrons.

NB: You are not expected to know about β^+ decay.

Question 68: C

Calculate the speed of the sound $= \frac{distance}{time} = \frac{500}{1.5} = 333\ ms^{-1}$

Thus, the $Wavelength = \frac{Speed}{Frequency} = \frac{333}{440}$

Approximate 333 to 330 to give: $\frac{330}{440} = \frac{3}{4} = 0.75\ m$

Question 69: B

Firstly, note the all the answer options are a magnitude of 10 apart. Thus, you don't have to worry about getting the correct numbers as long as you get the correct power of 10. You can therefore make your life easier by rounding, e.g. approximate π to 3, etc.

The area of the shell = πr^2.

$= \pi \times (50 \times 10^{-3})^2 = \pi \times (5 \times 10^{-2})^2$

$= \pi \times 25 \times 10^{-4} = 7.5 \times 10^{-3}\ m^2$

The deceleration of the shell $= \frac{u-v}{t} = \frac{200}{500 \times 10^{-6}} = 0.4 \times 10^6\ ms^{-2}$

Then, using Newton's Second Law: $Braking\ force = mass \times acceleration = 1 \times 0.4 \times 10^6 = 4 \times 10^5 N$

Finally: $Pressure = \frac{Force}{Area} = \frac{4 \times 10^5}{7.5 \times 10^{-3}} = \frac{8}{15} \times 10^8\ Pa \approx 5 \times 10^7 Pa$

Question 70: B

The fountain transfers 10% of 1,000 J of energy per second into 120 litres of water per minute. Thus, it transfers 100 J into 2 litres of water per second. Therefore, the Total Gravitational Potential Energy, $E_p = mg\Delta h$

Thus, $100\,J = 2 \times 10 \times h$

Hence, $h = \frac{100}{20} = 5\ m$

Question 71: E

In step down transformers, the number of turns of the primary coil is larger than that of the secondary coil to decrease the voltage. If a transformer is 100% efficient, the electrical power input = electrical power output (P=IV).

Question 72: C

The percentage of C^{14} in the bone halves every 5,730 years. Since it has decreased from 100% to 6.25%, it has undergone 4 half-lives. Thus, the bone is 4 x 5,730 years old = 22,920 years.

Question 73: E

This is a straightforward question in principle, as it just requires you to plug the values into the equation: $Velocity = Wavelength \, x \, Frequency$ – Just ensure you work in SI units to get the correct answer.

$$Frequency = \frac{2\,m/s}{2.5\,m} = 0.8\,Hz = 0.8 \times 10^{-6} MHz = 8 \times 10^{-7}\,MHz$$

Question 74: E

If an element has a half-life of 25 days, its BQ value will be halved every 25 days.

A total of 350/25 = 14 half-lives have elapsed. Thus, the count rate has halved 14 times. Therefore, to calculate the original rate, the final count rate must be doubled 14 times = 50 x 2^{14}.

$2^{14} = 2^5 \times 2^5 \times 2^4 = 32 \times 32 \times 16 = 16{,}384$.

Therefore, the original count rate = 16,384 x 50 = 819,200

Question 75: D

Remember that $V = IR = \frac{P}{I}$ and $Power = \frac{Work\ Done}{Time} = \frac{Force\ x\ Distance}{Time} = Force\ x\ Velocity;$

Thus, A is derived from: $V = IR$, B is derived from: $= \frac{P}{I}$,

C is derived from: $Voltage = \frac{Power}{Current} = \frac{Force\ x\ Velocity}{Current}$,

Since $Charge = Current\ x\ Time$, E and F are derived from: $Voltage = \frac{Power}{Current} = \frac{Force\ x\ Distance}{Time\ x\ Current} = \frac{J}{As} = \frac{J}{C}$,

D is incorrect as Nm = J. Thus the correct variant would be NmC^{-1}

Question 76: E

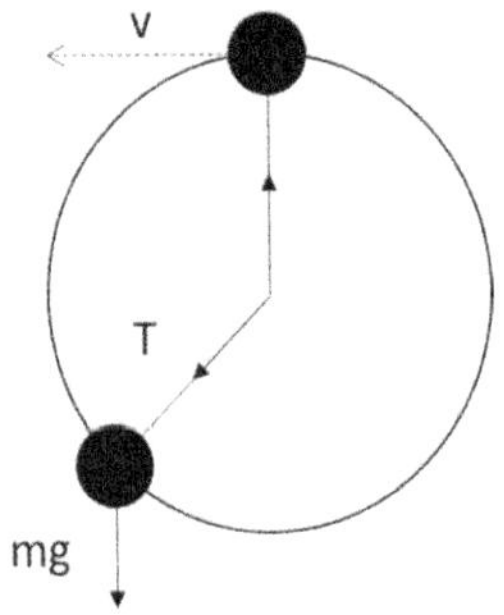

Forces on the ball are $weight = mg$ which is constant and tension T which varies with position.

$F = ma\ ;\ a = \frac{v^2}{r}$

$T + mg = m\frac{v^2}{r}$

If the ball stops moving in a circle it means there is no tension in the string (T=0) so: $mg = m\frac{v^2}{r}$

$v = \sqrt{gr}$

Question 77: E

To move at a steady velocity there is no acceleration, so the forces are balanced. Resolve along the slope: $F + mg\sin(30) = T\cos(30)$

$\frac{mg}{2} + F = \frac{T\sqrt{3}}{2}$

$T = \frac{2}{\sqrt{3}}\left(\frac{mg}{2} + F\right)$

Work done in pulling the box is W=Fd where the distance can be expressed as a function of velocity and time $d = v\Delta t$ so: $W = vF\Delta t$

Since power can expressed as $P = \frac{W}{\Delta t}$ we have $P = \frac{vF\Delta t}{\Delta t}$

$P = vT\cos(30)$

$P = \left(\frac{mg}{2} + F\right)v$

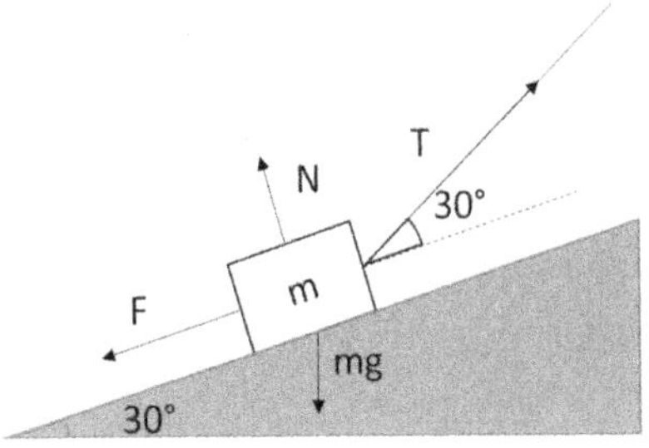

Question 78: C

This is a conservation of energy problem. In the absence of friction there is no dissipation of energy therefore the sum of the potential and kinetic energy must be constant: $\frac{1}{2}mv^2 + mgh = E$

At its highest the velocity and kinetic energy are 0 so $E = mgh_1$.
At the bottom of the swing the potential energy at h is converted to kinetic energy.

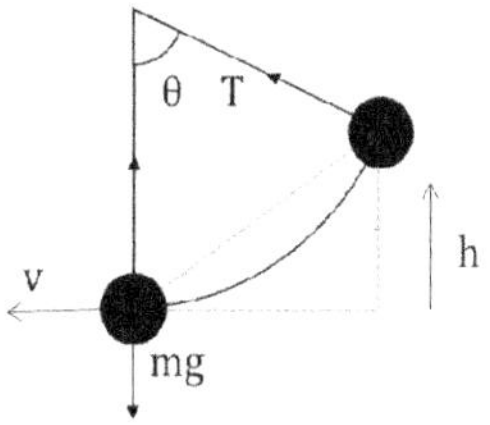

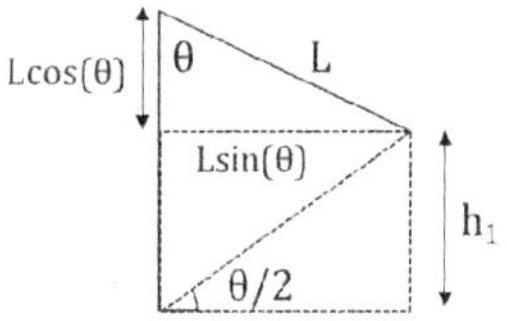

Therefore: $\frac{1}{2}mv^2 = E = mgh_1 \therefore v = \sqrt{2gh_1}$

$h_1 = l(1 - \cos(\theta))$

$v = \sqrt{2gh_1} = \sqrt{2gl(1 - \cos(\theta))}$

Question 79: E

Conservation of momentum. Before : $p = mu_1$

Afterward: $p = m(v_1 + v_2)$

Vertical components must cancel since spheres are moving in opposite directions therefore: $v_2 \sin(\theta) = 2v_2 \sin(30°)$

$\sin(\theta) = 1$ giving $\theta = 90°$

Question 80: D

This is a modified Newton's pendulum. Elastic collision means that both kinetic energy and momentum are conserved. Therefore three balls will swing at a velocity equal to the velocity of the first to conserve both momentum and kinetic energy.

$$\frac{1}{2}mv^2 = \frac{1}{2}m_2u^2$$

But momentum is also conserved so $mv = m_2u$

Mass must therefore be equal i.e. 3 balls move at a velocity $u = v$

Question 81: A

The ball will follow a parabolic trajectory. The minimum angle is therefore given by the gradient of the parabola which goes through the points (0,3) and (-6,0). [**NB:** do not use a triangle, the ball lands 6m behind the fence so it takes a parabolic trajectory with the vertex directly above the fence. The smallest possible initial angle places the ball just passing over the fence.]

$y = -ax^2 + 3$

$0 = -36a + 3$

$a = \frac{1}{12}$

$y = -\frac{x^2}{12} + 3$

$\frac{dy}{dx} = -\frac{2x}{12} = -\frac{x}{6}$

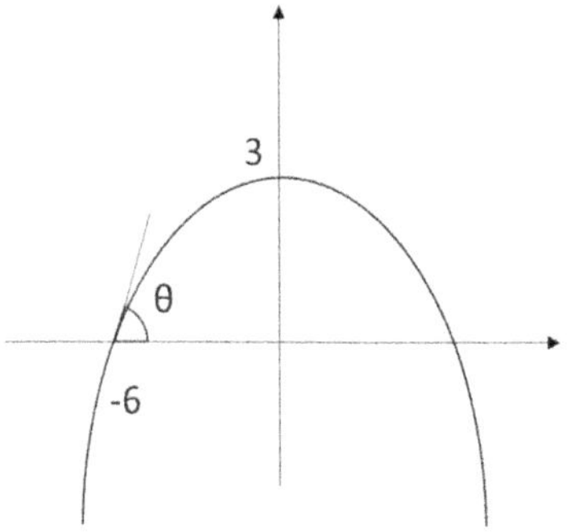

Question 82: B

Simple harmonic motion $m\frac{d^2x}{dt^2} = -kx$

Hence: $T \propto \sqrt{\frac{m}{k}}$.

Doubling k and halving m would therefore reduce time period T by a half. The frequency is the reciprocal of the time period and will therefore double.

Question 83: C

At the top of the bounce the kinetic energy is zero as velocity is zero. Highest velocity will be downwards before impact where $potential\ energy\ lost = kinetic\ energy\ gained$ (assuming no air resistance and therefore conservation of energy).

$\frac{1}{2}mv^2 = mgh$

Kinetic energy before hitting the ground:

E_k=m.10.3 = 30m

Highest velocity:
$v^2 = 2gh = 60$
$v = 2\sqrt{15}$

Question 84: D
Speed is close to c so need to consider Lorentz contraction in special relativity: $l' = l\sqrt{1 - \frac{v^2}{c^2}}$

$= l\sqrt{1 - \frac{\left(\frac{c}{10}\right)^2}{c^2}}$

$= l\sqrt{0.99}$

Question 85: B
Initial kinetic energy must equal work done to stop the car: $\frac{1}{2}mv^2 = Fd = \frac{mg}{2}d$
$v^2 = gd$
$d = \frac{v^2}{g}$

Question 86: D
Find the proportion of amplitude left, then use this to work out how many half-lives have passed: $\frac{25}{200} = \frac{1}{8} = \frac{1}{2^3}$
Therefore 12 seconds is three half-lives and $t_{1/2}$=4s.

Question 87: C
$f_{beats} = |f_1 - f_2| = \frac{1}{8}f = 10$
$f = 80$ Hz

Question 88: E

The two waves would interfere destructively as they are half a wavelength phase difference. A wave would reflect back onto itself in this way if reflected in a plane, perpendicular surface. These two waves travelling in opposite directions (incident and reflected) would produce a standing wave, with this exact point in time corresponding to zero amplitude. There are 5 nodes with two fixed ends making it the 4th harmonic of a standing wave. Thus, all the statements are true.

Question 89: C

Beta decay changes a neutron to a proton releasing an electron and an antineutrino (*a* doesn't change, *b* increases by one), then alpha decay emits an alpha particle which is two protons and two neutrons (*a* decreases by 4, *b* decreases by two).

Question 90: A

Assume ideal gas: $PV = nRT$

$$P_2 = \frac{nR2T}{1.1V}$$

Therefore change in P is equal to $\frac{2}{1.1} = 1.818$ which is an 82% increase.

Question 91: A

Alpha particles are +2 and are deflected to the right. Were they a -1 charge they would follow path Q however electrons have a far smaller mass and will be deflected much more than an alpha particle. Then the beam of electrons is more likely to follow path P.

Question 92: D

If brightness increases with current, each association can be analysed individually and remembering that all the bulbs are identical.

For the association of three bulbs in the parallel: since the three bulbs are in parallel with the source of energy, the current leaving the source will be equally divided between each one of them and equal to $I = \frac{V}{R}$For the association of three bulbs in series the same value of current passes throw three bulbs and is equal to the voltage divided by the total resistance $I = \frac{V}{3R}$

Finally, for the association of one bulb in parallel with two bulbs in series the current will be divided to the total resistance of each branch.

For two in series and one in parallel, the two in series have resistance 2R so:

$$\frac{1}{R_T} = \frac{1}{2R} + \frac{1}{R} \therefore R_T = \frac{2R}{3}$$

$$I_T = \frac{V}{R_T} = \frac{3V}{2R}$$

This is split with a third going to the branch with resistance 2R and two thirds going to the branch with resistance R: $I_6 = \frac{V}{R}$; $I_{4,5} = \frac{V}{2R}$

Current in 1,2,3 and 6 is the same and is the greatest

Question 93: A

Object is between f and the lens, so rays will diverge on the other side producing a virtual image on the same side which is magnified.

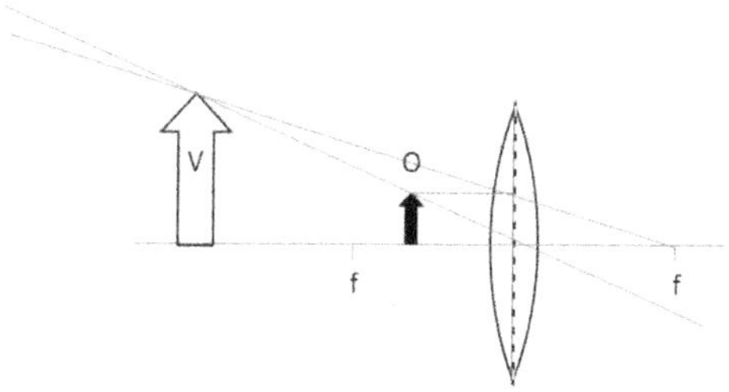

Question 94: B

Moments taken with the pivot at the wall must balance therefore: $\frac{2}{3} lT \sin\theta = lmg$

$$T = \frac{3mg}{2\sin\theta}$$

Question 95: C

This process is known as the photoelectric effect (photons producing electron emission) and the presence of a work function arises due to wave particle duality. [n.b. thermionic emission uses heat not incident radiation to emit particles]. As the axis is kinetic energy and not potential, the intercept is the work function not the stopping potential.

Question 96: D

Huygens' principle states that every point on a wavefront is like a point source of a wave travelling at the same speed. This explains the first four but does not account for energy loss during propagation i.e. damping.

Question 97: A

Carnot cycle is the most efficient where: $\eta = \frac{work\ done}{heat\ put\ in} = 1 - \frac{T_{cold}}{T_{hot}} = 1 - \frac{240}{420} = \frac{3}{7} \approx 43\%$

Question 98: B

B is the only correct statement. NB- while generators can have a moving coil, they could equally have a moving magnetic field instead, so this is not true.

Question 99: C

NAND (gives X), OR (gives Y) and AND (gives Z) gates

Question 100: E

Several almost synonymous terms. Those in bold are correct. E is the only line with all three.

	P	Q	R
A	**Elastic Modulus**	**Yield stress**	Fracture toughness
B	**Tensile Modulus**	**Plastic onset**	Yield stress
C	Hardness	**Stiffness**	**Ductile failure**
D	Ductility	**Elastic limit**	Brittle fracture
E	**Young's Modulus**	**Yield stress**	**Fracture stress**

Question 101: B

Each three-block combination is mutually exclusive to any other combination, so the probabilities are added. Each block pick is independent of all other picks, so the probabilities can be multiplied. For this scenario there are three possible combinations:

P(2 red blocks and 1 yellow block) = P(red then red then yellow) + P(red then yellow then red) + P(yellow then red then red) =

$(\frac{12}{20} \text{ x} \frac{11}{19} \text{ x} \frac{8}{18}) + (\frac{12}{20} \text{ x} \frac{8}{19} \text{ x} \frac{11}{18}) + (\frac{8}{20} \text{ x} \frac{12}{19} \text{ x} \frac{11}{18}) =$

$\frac{3 \text{ x } 12 \text{ x } 11 \text{ x } 8}{20 \text{ x } 19 \text{ x } 18} = \frac{44}{95}$

Question 102: C

Multiply through by 15: $3(3x + 5) + 5(2x - 2) = 18 \text{ x } 15$

Thus: $9x + 15 + 10x - 10 = 270$

$9x + 10x = 270 - 15 + 10$

$19x = 265$

$x = 13.95$

Question 103: C

This is a rare case where you need to factorise a complex polynomial:

(3x)(x) = 0, possible pairs: 2 x 10, 10 x 2, 4 x 5, 5 x 4

(3x - 4)(x + 5) = 0

3x - 4 = 0, so $x = \frac{4}{3}$

x + 5 = 0, so x = -5

Question 104: C

$$\frac{5(x-4)}{(x+2)(x-4)} + \frac{3(x+2)}{(x+2)(x-4)}$$

$$= \frac{5x-20+3x+6}{(x+2)(x-4)}$$

$$= \frac{8x-14}{(x+2)(x-4)}$$

Question 105: E

$p \propto \sqrt[3]{q}$, so $p = k\sqrt[3]{q}$

p = 12 when q = 27 gives $12 = k\sqrt[3]{27}$, so 12 = 3k and k = 4

so $p = 4\sqrt[3]{q}$

Now p = 24:

$24 = 4\sqrt[3]{q}$, so $6 = \sqrt[3]{q}$ and $q = 6^3 = 216$

Question 106: A

8 x 9 = 72

8 = (4 x 2) = 2 x 2 x 2

9 = 3 x 3

$(2 \times 2 \times 2 \times 3 \times 3)^2 = 2 \times 2 \times 2 \times 2 \times 2 \times 2 \times 3 \times 3 \times 3 \times 3 = 2^6 \times 3^4$

Question 107: C

Note that 1.151 x 2 = 2.302.

Thus: $\frac{2\,x\,10^5 + 2\,x\,10^2}{10^{10}} = 2\,x\,10^{-5} + 2\,x\,10^{-8}$

$= 0.00002 + 0.00000002 = 0.00002002$

Question 108: E

$y^2 + ay + b$

$= (y+2)^2 - 5 = y^2 + 4y + 4 - 5$

$= y^2 + 4y + 4 - 5 = y^2 + 4y - 1$

So a = 4 and y = -1

Question 109: E

Take $5(m+4n)$ as a common factor to give: $\frac{4(m+4n)}{5(m+4n)} + \frac{5(m-2n)}{5(m+4n)}$

Simplify to give: $\frac{4m+16n+5m-10n}{5(m+4n)} = \frac{9m+6n}{5(m+4n)} = \frac{3(3m+2n)}{5(m+4n)}$

Question 110: C

$A\,\alpha\,\frac{1}{\sqrt{B}}$. Thus, $= \frac{k}{\sqrt{B}}$.

Substitute the values in to give: $4 = \frac{k}{\sqrt{25}}$.

Thus, $k = 20$.

Therefore, $A = \frac{20}{\sqrt{B}}$.

When B = 16, $A = \frac{20}{\sqrt{16}} = \frac{20}{4} = 5$

Question 111: E

Angles SVU and STU are opposites and add up to 180°, so STU = 91°

The angle of the centre of a circle is twice the angle at the circumference so SOU = 2 x 91° = 182°

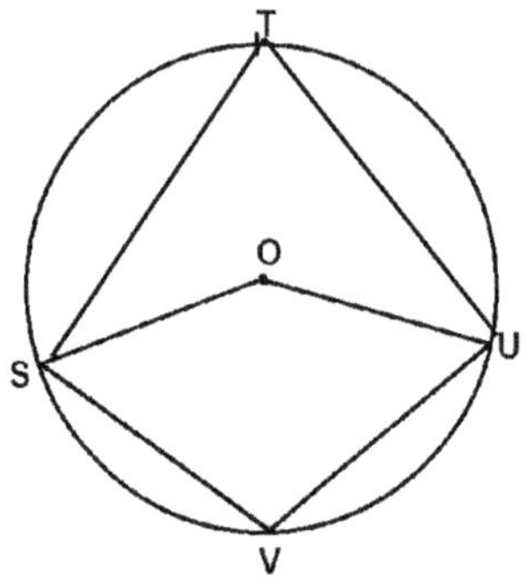

Question 112: E

The surface area of an open cylinder A = 2πrh. Cylinder B is an enlargement of A, so the increases in radius (r) and height (h) will be proportional: $\frac{r_A}{r_B} = \frac{h_A}{h_B}$. Let us call the proportion coefficient n, where n = $\frac{r_A}{r_B} = \frac{h_A}{h_B}$.

So $\frac{Area\ A}{Area\ B} = \frac{2\pi r_A h_A}{2\pi r_B h_B} = n\ x\ n = n^2$. $\frac{Area\ A}{Area\ B} = \frac{32\pi}{8\pi} = 4$, so n = 2.

The proportion coefficient n = 2 also applies to their volumes, where the third dimension (also radius, i.e. the r^2 in $V = \pi r^2 h$) is equally subject to this constant of proportionality. The cylinder's volumes are related by $n^3 = 8$.

If the smaller cylinder has volume 2π cm^3, then the larger will have volume $2\pi \times n^3 = 2\pi \times 8 = 16\pi\ cm^3$.

Question 113: E

$= \frac{8}{x(3-x)} - \frac{6(3-x)}{x(3-x)}$

$= \frac{8-18+6x}{x(3-x)}$

$= \frac{6x-10}{x(3-x)}$

Question 114: B

For the black ball to be drawn in the last round, white balls must be drawn every round. Thus the probability is given by $P = \frac{9}{10} \text{ X } \frac{8}{9} \text{X } \frac{7}{8} \text{X } \frac{6}{7} \text{X } \frac{5}{6} \text{X } \frac{4}{5} \text{X } \frac{3}{4} \text{X } \frac{2}{3} \text{X } \frac{1}{2}$

$= \frac{9 \text{ x } 8 \text{ x } 7 \text{ x } 6 \text{ x } 5 \text{ x } 4 \text{ x } 3 \text{ x } 2 \text{ x } 1}{10 \text{ x } 9 \text{ x } 8 \text{ x } 7 \text{ x } 6 \text{ x } 5 \text{ x } 4 \text{ x } 3 \text{ x } 2 \text{ x } 1} = \frac{1}{10}$

Question 115: C

The probability of getting a king the first time is $\frac{4}{52} = \frac{1}{13}$, and the probability of getting a king the second time is $\frac{3}{51}$. These are independent events thus, the probability of drawing two kings is $\frac{1}{13} x \frac{3}{51} = \frac{3}{663} = \frac{1}{221}$

Question 116: B

The probabilities of all outcomes must sum to one, so if the probability of rolling a 1 is x, then: $x + x + x + x + 2x = 1$. Therefore, $x = \frac{1}{7}$.

The probability of obtaining two sixes $P_{12} = \frac{2}{7} \text{ X} \frac{2}{7} = \frac{4}{49}$

Question 117: B

There are plenty of ways of counting, however the easiest is as follows: 0 is divisible by both 2 and 3. Half of the numbers from 1 to 36 are even (i.e. 18 of them). 3, 9, 15, 21, 27, 33 are the only numbers divisible by 3 that we've missed. There are 25 outcomes divisible by 2 or 3, out of 37.

Question 118: C

List the six ways of achieving this outcome: HHTT, HTHT, HTTH, TTHH, THTH and THHT. There are 2^4 possible outcomes for 4 consecutive coin flips, so the probability of two heads and two tails is: $6 x \frac{1}{2^4} = \frac{6}{16} = \frac{3}{8}$

Question 119: D

Count the number of ways to get a 5, 6 or 7 (draw the square if helpful). The ways to get a 5 are: 1, 4; 2, 3; 3, 2; 4, 1. The ways to get a 6 are: 1, 5; 2, 4; 3, 3; 4, 2; 5, 1. The ways to get a 7 are: 1, 6; 2, 5; 3, 4; 4, 3; 5, 2; 6, 1. That is 15 out of 36 possible outcomes.

	1	2	3	4	5	6
1	2	3	4	5	6	7
2	3	4	5	6	7	8
3	4	5	6	7	8	9
4	5	6	7	8	9	10
5	6	7	8	9	10	11
6	7	8	9	10	11	12

Question 120: C

There are x+y+z balls in the bag, and the probability of picking a red ball is $\frac{x}{(x+y+z)}$ and the probability of picking a green ball is $\frac{z}{(x+y+z)}$. These are independent events, so the probability of picking red then green is $\frac{xz}{(x+y+z)^2}$ and the probability of picking green then red is the same. These outcomes are mutually exclusive, so are added.

Question 121: B

There are two ways of doing it, pulling out a red ball then a blue ball, or pulling out a blue ball and then a red ball. Let us work out the probability of the first: $\frac{x}{(x+y+z)} \times \frac{y}{x+y+z-1}$, and the probability of the second option will be the same. These are mutually exclusive options, so the probabilities may be summed.

Question 122: A

[x: Player 1 wins point, y: Player 2 wins point]

Player 1 wins in five rounds if we get: yxxxx, xyxxx, xxyxx, xxxyx.

(Note the case of xxxxy would lead to player 1 winning in 4 rounds, which the question forbids.)

Each of these have a probability of $p^4(1-p)$. Thus, the solution is $4p^4(1-p)$.

Question 123: F

$4x + 7 + 18x + 20 = 14$

$22x + 27 = 14$

Thus, $22x = -13$

Giving $x = -\frac{13}{22}$

Question 124: D

$r^3 = \frac{3V}{4\pi}$

Thus, $r = \left(\frac{3V}{4\pi}\right)^{1/3}$

Therefore, S = $4\pi\left[\left(\frac{3V}{4\pi}\right)^{\frac{1}{3}}\right]^2 = 4\pi\left(\frac{3V}{4\pi}\right)^{\frac{2}{3}}$

$= \frac{4\pi(3V)^{\frac{2}{3}}}{(4\pi)^{\frac{2}{3}}} = (3V)^{\frac{2}{3}} \text{ x } \frac{(4\pi)^1}{(4\pi)^{\frac{2}{3}}}$

$= (3V)^{\frac{2}{3}}\,(4\pi)^{1-\frac{2}{3}} = (4\pi)^{\frac{1}{3}}(3V)^{\frac{2}{3}}$

Question 125: A

Let each unit length be x.

Thus, $S = 6x^2$. Therefore, $x = \left(\frac{S}{6}\right)^{\frac{1}{2}}$

V = x^3. Thus, $V = [\left(\frac{S}{6}\right)^{\frac{1}{2}}]^3$ so $V = \left(\frac{S}{6}\right)^{\frac{3}{2}}$

Question 126: B

Multiplying the second equation by 2 we get 4x + 16y = 24. Subtracting the first equation from this we get 13y = 17, so y = $\frac{17}{13}$. Then solving for x we get x = $\frac{10}{13}$. You could also try substituting possible solutions one by one, although given that the equations are both linear and contain easy numbers, it is quicker to solve them algebraically.

Question 127: A

Multiply by the denominator to give: $(7x + 10) = (3y^2 + 2)(9x + 5)$

Partially expand brackets on right side: $(7x + 10) = 9x(3y^2 + 2) + 5(3y^2 + 2)$

Take x terms across to left side: $7x - 9x(3y^2 + 2) = 5(3y^2 + 2) - 10$

Take x outside the brackets: $x[7 - 9(3y^2 + 2)] = 5(3y^2 + 2) - 10$

Thus: $x = \frac{5(3y^2 + 2) - 10}{7 - 9(3y^2 + 2)}$

Simplify to give: $x = \frac{(15y^2)}{(7 - 9(3y^2 + 2))}$

Question 128: F

$$3x\left(\frac{3x^7}{x^{\frac{1}{3}}}\right)^3 = 3x\left(\frac{3^3x^{21}}{x^{\frac{3}{3}}}\right)$$

$$= 3x\,\frac{27x^{21}}{x} = 81x^{21}$$

Question 129: D

$$2x[2^{\frac{7}{14}}\,x^{\frac{7}{14}}] = 2x[2^{\frac{1}{2}}\,x^{\frac{1}{2}}]$$

$$= 2x(\sqrt{2}\,\sqrt{x}) = 2\,[\sqrt{x}\sqrt{x}][\sqrt{2}\,\sqrt{x}]$$

$$= 2\sqrt{2x^3}$$

Question 130: A

$A = \pi r^2$, therefore $10\pi = \pi r^2$

Thus, $r = \sqrt{10}$

Therefore, the circumference is $2\pi\sqrt{10}$

Question 131: D

$3.4 = 12 + (3 + 4) = 19$

$19.5 = 95 + (19 + 5) = 119$

Question 132: D

$$2.3 = \frac{2^3}{2} = 4$$

$$4.2 = \frac{4^2}{4} = 4$$

Question 133: F

This is a tricky question that requires you to know how to 'complete the square':

$(x + 1.5)(x + 1.5) = x^2 + 3x + 2.25$

Thus, $(x + 1.5)^2 - 7.25 = x^2 + 3x - 5 = 0$

Therefore, $(x + 1.5)^2 = 7.25 = \frac{29}{4}$

Thus, $x + 1.5 = \sqrt{\frac{29}{4}}$

Thus $x = -\frac{3}{2} \pm \sqrt{\frac{29}{4}} = -\frac{3}{2} \pm \frac{\sqrt{29}}{2}$

Question 134: B

Whilst you definitely need to solve this graphically, it is necessary to complete the square for the first equation to allow you to draw it more easily:

$(x+2)^2 = x^2 + 4x + 4$

Thus, $y = (x+2)^2 + 10 = x^2 + 4x + 14$

This is now an easy curve to draw ($y = x^2$ that has moved 2 units left and 10 units up). The turning point of this quadratic is to the left and well above anything in x^3, so the only solution is the first intersection of the two curves in the upper right quadrant around (3.4, 39).

Question 135: C

By far the easiest way to solve this is to sketch them (don't waste time solving them algebraically). As soon as you've done this, it'll be very obvious that y = 2 and $y = 1-x^2$ don't intersect, since the latter has its turning point at (0, 1) and zero points at x = -1 and 1. y = x and $y = x^2$ intersect at the origin and (1, 1), and y = 2 runs through both.

Question 136: B

Notice that you're not required to get the actual values – just the number's magnitude. Thus, 897653 can be approximated to 900,000 and 0.009764 to 0.01. Therefore, 900,000 x 0.01 = 9,000

Question 137: C

Multiply through by 70: $7(7x+3)+10(3x+1) = 14 \times 70$

Simplify: $49x + 21 + 30x + 10 = 980$

$79x + 31 = 980$

$x = \frac{949}{79}$

Question 138: A

Split the equilateral triangle into 2 right-angled triangles and apply Pythagoras' theorem:

$x^2 = \left(\frac{x}{2}\right)^2 + h^2$. Thus $h^2 = \frac{3}{4}x^2$

$h = \sqrt{\frac{3x^2}{4}} = \frac{\sqrt{3x^2}}{2}$

The area of a triangle = ½ x base x height = $\frac{1}{2} x \frac{\sqrt{3x^2}}{2}$

Simplifying gives: $x\frac{\sqrt{3x^2}}{4} = x\frac{\sqrt{3}\sqrt{x^2}}{4} = \frac{x^2\sqrt{3}}{4}$

Question 139: A

This is a question testing your ability to spot 'the difference between two squares.'

Factorise to give: $3 - \frac{7x(5x-1)(5x+1)}{(7x)^2(5x+1)}$

Cancel out: $3 - \frac{(5x-1)}{7x}$

Question 140: C

The easiest way to do this is to 'complete the square':

$(x - 5)^2 = x^2 - 10x + 25$

Thus, $(x - 5)^2 - 125 = x^2 - 10x - 100 = 0$

Therefore, $(x - 5)^2 = 125$

$x - 5 = \pm\sqrt{125} = \pm\sqrt{25}\sqrt{5} = \pm 5\sqrt{5}$

$x = 5 \pm 5\sqrt{5}$

Question 141: B

Factorise by completing the square:

$x^2 - 4x + 7 = (x - 2)^2 + 3$

Simplify: $(x - 2)^2 = y^3 + 2 - 3$

$x - 2 = \pm\sqrt{y^3 - 1}$

$x = 2 \pm \sqrt{y^3 - 1}$

Question 142: D

Square both sides to give: $(3x + 2)^2 = 7x^2 + 2x + y$

Thus: $y = (3x + 2)^2 - 7x^2 - 2x = (9x^2 + 12x + 4) - 7x^2 - 2x$

$y = 2x^2 + 10x + 4$

Question 143: C

This is a fourth order polynomial, which you aren't expected to be able to factorise at GCSE. This is where looking at the options makes your life a lot easier. In all of them, opening the bracket on the right side involves making $(y \pm 1)^4$ on the left side, i.e. the answers are hinting that $(y \pm 1)^4$ is the solution to the fourth order polynomial.

Since there are negative terms in the equations (e.g. $-4y^3$), the solution has to be:

$(y-1)^4 = y^4 - 4y^3 + 6y^2 - 4y + 1$

Therefore, $(y-1)^4 + 1 = x^5 + 7$

Thus, $y - 1 = (x^5 + 6)^{\frac{1}{4}}$

$y = 1 + (x^5 + 6)^{1/4}$

Question 144: A

Let the width of the television be 4x and the height of the television be 3x.

Then by Pythagoras: $(4x)^2 + (3x)^2 = 50^2$

Simplify: $25x^2 = 2500$

Thus: $x = 10$. Therefore: the screen is 30 inches by 40 inches, i.e. the area is 1,200 inches^2.

Question 145: C

Square both sides to give: $1 + \frac{3}{x^2} = (y^5 + 1)^2$

Multiply out: $\frac{3}{x^2} = (y^{10} + 2y^5 + 1) - 1$

Thus: $x^2 = \frac{3}{y^{10}+2y^5}$

Therefore: $x = \sqrt{\frac{3}{y^{10} + 2y^5}}$

Question 146: C

The easiest way is to double the first equation and triple the second to get:

$6x - 10y = 20 \text{ and } 6x + 6y = 39$.

Subtract the first from the second to give: $16y = 19$,

Therefore, $y = \frac{19}{16}$.

Substitute back into the first equation to give $x = \frac{85}{16}$.

Question 147: C

This is fairly straightforward; the first inequality is the easier one to work with: B and D and E violate it, so we just need to check A and C in the second inequality.

C: $1^3 - 2^2 < 3$, but A: $2^3 - 1^2 > 3$

Question 148: B

Whilst this can be done graphically, it's quicker to do algebraically (because the second equation is not as easy to sketch). Intersections occur where the curves have the same coordinates.

Thus: $x + 4 = 4x^2 + 5x + 5$

Simplify: $4x^2 + 4x + 1 = 0$

Factorise: $(2x + 1)(2x + 1) = 0$

Thus, the two graphs only intersect once at $x = -\frac{1}{2}$

Question 149: D

It's better to do this algebraically as the equations are easy to work with and you would need to sketch very accurately to get the answer. Intersections occur where the curves have the same coordinates. Thus: $x^3 = x$

$x^3 - x = 0$

Thus: $x(x^2 - 1) = 0$

Spot the 'difference between two squares': $x(x+1)(x-1) = 0$

Thus, there are 3 intersections: at $x = 0, 1 \text{ and } -1$

Question 150: E

Note that the line is the hypotenuse of a right angled triangle with one side unit length and one side of length ½. By Pythagoras, $\left(\frac{1}{2}\right)^2 + 1^2 = x^2$

Thus, $x^2 = \frac{1}{4} + 1 = \frac{5}{4}$

$$x = \sqrt{\frac{5}{4}} = \frac{\sqrt{5}}{\sqrt{4}} = \frac{\sqrt{5}}{2}$$

Question 151: D

We can eliminate z from equation (1) and (2) by multiplying equation (1) by 3 and adding it to equation (2):

$3x + 3y - 3z = -3$	Equation (1) multiplied by 3
$2x - 2y + 3z = 8$	Equation (2) then add both equations
$5x + y = 5$	We label this as equation (4)

Now we must eliminate the same variable z from another pair of equations by using equation (1) and (3):

$2x + 2y - 2z = -2$	Equation (1) multiplied by 2
$2x - y + 2z = 9$	Equation (3) then add both equations
$4x + y = 7$	We label this as equation (5)

We now use both equations (4) and (5) to obtain the value of x:

$5x + y = 5$	Equation (4)
$-4x - y = -7$	Equation (5) multiplied by -1
$x = -2$	

Substitute x back in to calculate y:

$4x + y = 7$

$4(-2) + y = 7$

$-8 + y = 7$

$y = 15$

Substitute x and y back in to calculate z:

$x + y - z = -1$

$-2 + 15 - z = -1$

$13 - z = -1$

$-z = -14$

$z = 14$

Thus: $x = -2$, $y = 15$, $z = 14$

Question 152: D

This is one of the easier maths questions. Take 3a as a factor to give:

$3a(a^2 - 10a + 25) = 3a(a - 5)(a - 5) = 3a(a - 5)^2$

Question 153: B

Note that 12 is the Lowest Common Multiple of 3 and 4. Thus:

$-3(4x + 3y) = -3(48)$ Multiply each side by -3

$4(3x + 2y) = 4(34)$ Multiply each side by 4

$-12x - 9y = -144$

$\underline{12x + 8y = 136}$ Add together

$-y = -8$

$y = 8$

Substitute y back in:

$4x + 3y = 48$

$4x + 3(8) = 48$

$4x + 24 = 48$

$4x = 24$

$x = 6$

Question 154: E

Don't be fooled, this is an easy question, just obey BODMAS and don't skip steps.

$\frac{-(25-28)^2}{-36+14} = \frac{-(-3)^2}{-22}$

This gives: $\frac{-(9)}{-22} = \frac{9}{22}$

Question 155: E

Since there are 26 possible letters for each of the 3 letters in the license plate, and there are 10 possible numbers (0-9) for each of the 3 numbers in the same plate, then the number of license plates would be:

(26) x (26) x (26) x (10) x (10) x (10) = 17,576,000

Question 156: B

Expand the brackets to give: $4x^2 - 12x + 9 = 0$.

Factorise: $(2x - 3)(2x - 3) = 0$.

Thus, only one solution exists, x = 1.5.

Note that you could also use the fact that the discriminant, $b^2 - 4ac = 0$ to get the answer.

Question 157: C

$$= \left(x^{\frac{1}{2}}\right)^{\frac{1}{2}} (y^{-3})^{\frac{1}{2}}$$

$$= x^{\frac{1}{4}} y^{-\frac{3}{2}} = \frac{x^{\frac{1}{4}}}{y^{\frac{3}{2}}}$$

Question 158: A

Let x, y, and z represent the rent for the 1-bedroom, 2-bedroom, and 3-bedroom flats, respectively. We can write 3 different equations: 1 for the rent, 1 for the repairs, and the last one for the statement that the 3-bedroom unit costs twice as much as the 1-bedroom unit.

(1) $x + y + z = 1240$

(2) $0.1x + 0.2y + 0.3z = 276$

(3) $z = 2x$

Substitute $z = 2x$ in both of the two other equations to eliminate z:

(4) $x + y + 2x = 3x + y = 1240$

(5) $0.1x + 0.2y + 0.3(2x) = 0.7x + 0.2y = 276$

$-2(3x + y) = -2(1240)$	Multiply each side of (4) by -2
$10(0.7x + 0.2y) = 10(276)$	Multiply each side of (5) by 10
(6) $-6x - 2y = -2480$	Add these 2 equations
<u>**(7)** $7x + 2y = 2760$</u>	
$x = 280$	
$z = 2(280) = 560$	Because $z = 2x$
$280 + y + 560 = 1240$	Because $x + y + z = 1240$
$y = 400$	

Thus, the units rent for £ 280, £ 400, £ 560 per week respectively.

Question 159: C

Following BODMAS:

$$= 5\left[5(6^2 - 5 \text{ x } 3) + 400^{\frac{1}{2}}\right]^{1/3} + 7$$

$$= 5\,[5(36 - 15) + 20]^{\frac{1}{3}} + 7$$

$$= 5\,[5(21) + 20]^{\frac{1}{3}} + 7$$

$$= 5\,(105 + 20)^{\frac{1}{3}} + 7$$

$$= 5\,(125)^{\frac{1}{3}} + 7$$

$$= 5\,(5) + 7$$

$$= 25 + 7 = 32$$

Question 160: B

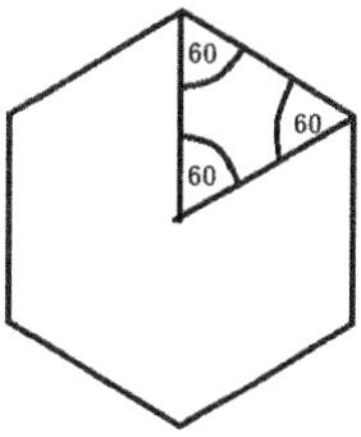

Consider a triangle formed by joining the centre to two adjacent vertices. Six similar triangles can be made around the centre – thus, the central angle is 60 degrees. Since the two lines forming the triangle are of equal length, we have 6 identical equilateral triangles in the hexagon.

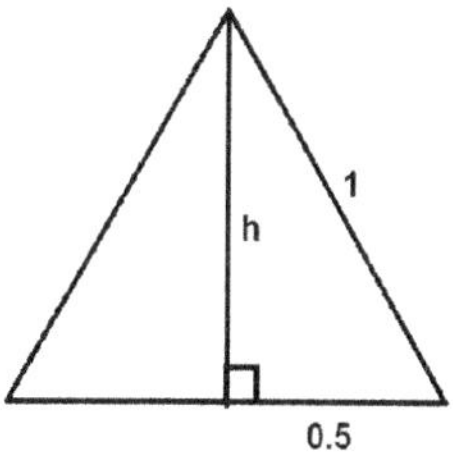

Now split the triangle in half and apply Pythagoras' theorem: $1^2 = 0.5^2 + h^2$

Thus, $h = \sqrt{\frac{3}{4}} = \frac{\sqrt{3}}{2}$

Thus, the area of the triangle is: $\frac{1}{2}bh = \frac{1}{2} \text{ x } 1 \text{ x} \frac{\sqrt{3}}{2} = \frac{\sqrt{3}}{4}$

Therefore, the area of the hexagon is: $\frac{\sqrt{3}}{4} \text{ x } 6 = \frac{3\sqrt{3}}{2}$

Question 161: B

Let x be the width and x+19 be the length.

Thus, the area of a rectangle is $x(x + 19) = 780$.

Therefore:

$x^2 + 19x - 780 = 0$

$(x - 20)(x + 39) = 0$

$x - 20 = 0$ or $x + 39 = 0$

$x = 20$ or $x = -39$

Since length can never be a negative number, we disregard $x = -39$ and use $x = 20$ instead.

Thus, the width is 20 metres and the length is 39 metres.

Question 162: B

The quickest way to solve is by trial and error, substituting the provided options. However, if you're keen to do this algebraically, you can do the following:

Start by setting up the equations: Perimeter = $2L + 2W = 34$

Thus: $L + W = 17$

Using Pythagoras: $L^2 + W^2 = 13^2$

Since $L + W = 17$, $W = 17 - L$

Therefore: $L^2 + (17 - L)^2 = 169$

$L^2 + 289 - 34L + L^2 = 169$

$2L^2 - 34L + 120 = 0$

$L^2 - 17L + 60 = 0$

$(L - 5)(L - 12) = 0$

Thus: $L = 5$ and $L = 12$

And: $W = 12$ and $W = 5$

Question 163: C

Multiply both sides by 8:	$4(3x - 5) + 2(x + 5) = 8(x + 1)$
Remove brackets:	$12x - 20 + 2x + 10 = 8x + 8$
Simplify:	$14x - 10 = 8x + 8$
Add 10:	$14x = 8x + 18$
Subtract 8x:	$6x = 18$
Therefore:	$x = 3$

Question 164: C

Recognise that 1.742 x 3 is 5.226. Now, the original equation simplifies to:

$$= \frac{3 \times 10^6 + 3 \times 10^5}{10^{10}}$$

$$= 3 \times 10^{-4} + 3 \times 10^{-5} = 3.3 \times 10^{-4}$$

Question 165: A

$$Area = \frac{(2+\sqrt{2})(4-\sqrt{2})}{2}$$

$$= \frac{8 - 2\sqrt{2} + 4\sqrt{2} - 2}{2}$$

$$= \frac{6 + 2\sqrt{2}}{2}$$

$$= 3 + \sqrt{2}$$

Question 166: C

Square both sides: $\frac{4}{x} + 9 = (y-2)^2$

$\frac{4}{x} = (y-2)^2 - 9$

Cross Multiply: $\frac{x}{4} = \frac{1}{(y-2)^2-9}$

$x = \frac{4}{y^2-4y+4-9}$

Factorise: $x = \frac{4}{y^2-4y-5}$

$x = \frac{4}{(y+1)(y-5)}$

Question 167: D

Set up the equation: $5x - 5 = 0.5(6x + 2)$

$10x - 10 = 6x + 2$

$4x = 12$

$x = 3$

Question 168: C

Round numbers appropriately: $\frac{55 + (\frac{9}{4})^2}{\sqrt{900}} = \frac{55 + \frac{81}{16}}{30}$

81 rounds to 80 to give: $\frac{55+5}{30} = \frac{60}{30} = 2$

Question 169: D

There are three outcomes from choosing the type of cheese in the crust. For each of the additional toppings to possibly add, there are 2 outcomes: 1 to include and another not to include a certain topping, for each of the 7 toppings

Thus, the number of different kinds of pizza is: 3 x 2 x 2 x 2 x 2 x 2 x 2 x 2

$= 3 \times 2^7$

$= 3 \times 128 = 384$

Question 170: A

Although it is possible to do this algebraically, by far the easiest way is via trial and error. The clue that you shouldn't attempt it algebraically is the fact that rearranging the first equation to make x or y the subject leaves you with a difficult equation to work with (e.g. $x = \sqrt{1 - y^2}$) when you try to substitute in the second.

An exceptionally good student might notice that the equations are symmetric in x and y, i.e. the solution is when x = y. Thus $2x^2 = 1$ and $2x = \sqrt{2}$ which gives $\frac{\sqrt{2}}{2}$ as the answer.

Question 171: C

If two shapes are congruent, then they are the same size and shape. Thus, congruent objects can be rotations and mirror images of each other. The two triangles in E are indeed congruent (SAS). Congruent objects must, by definition, have the same angles.

Question 172: B

Rearrange the equation: $x^2 + x - 6 \geq 0$

Factorise: $(x + 3)(x - 2) \geq 0$

Remember that this is a quadratic inequality so requires a quick sketch to ensure you don't make a silly mistake with which way the sign is.

$y = 0$ when $x = 2$ and $x = -3$.

y > 0 when $x > 2$ or $x < -3$.

Thus, $x \leq -3$ *and* $x \geq 2$.

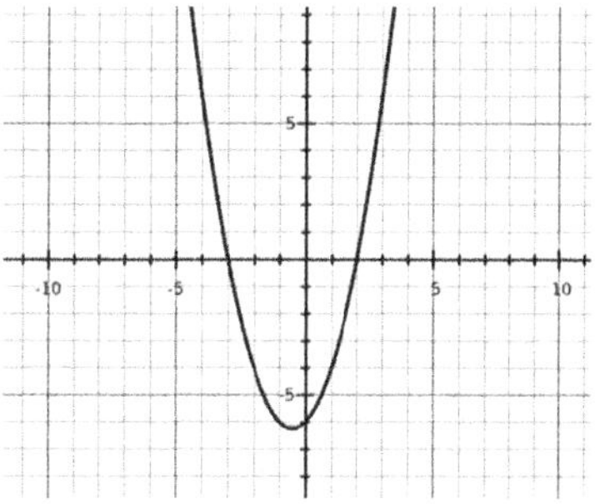

Question 173: B

Using Pythagoras: $a^2 + b^2 = x^2$

Since the triangle is equilateral: $a = b,\ so\ 2a^2 = x^2$

Area $= \frac{1}{2} base\ x\ height = \frac{1}{2}a^2$. From above, $a^2 = \frac{x^2}{2}$

Thus, the area $= \frac{1}{2} x \frac{x^2}{2} = \frac{x^2}{4}$

Question 174: A

If X and Y are doubled, the value of Q increases by 4. Halving the value of A reduces this to 2. Finally, tripling the value of B reduces this to ⅔, i.e. the value decreases by ⅓.

Question 175: C

The quickest way to do this is to sketch the curves. This requires you to factorise both equations by completing the square:

$x^2 - 2x + 3 = (x-1)^2 + 2$

$x^2 - 6x - 10 = (x-3)^2 - 19$ Thus, the first equation has a turning point at (1, 2) and doesn't cross the x-axis. The second equation has a turning point at (3, -19) and crosses the x-axis twice.

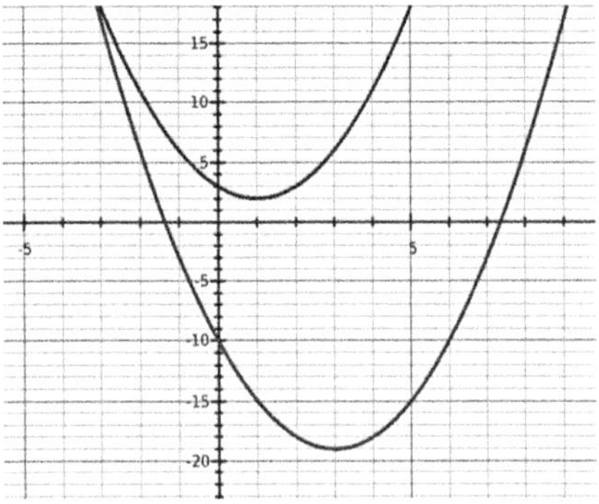

Question 176: C

Segment area $= \frac{60}{360}\pi r^2 = \frac{1}{6}\pi r^2$

$\frac{x}{\sin 30^\circ} = \frac{2r}{\sin 60^\circ}$

$x = \frac{2r}{\sqrt{3}}$

Total triangle area$= 2 \times \frac{1}{2} \times \frac{2r}{\sqrt{3}} \times 2r = \frac{4r^2}{\sqrt{3}}$

Proportion covered: $\frac{1}{6}\pi r^2 \Big/ \frac{4r^2}{\sqrt{3}} = \frac{\sqrt{3}\pi}{24} \approx 23\%$

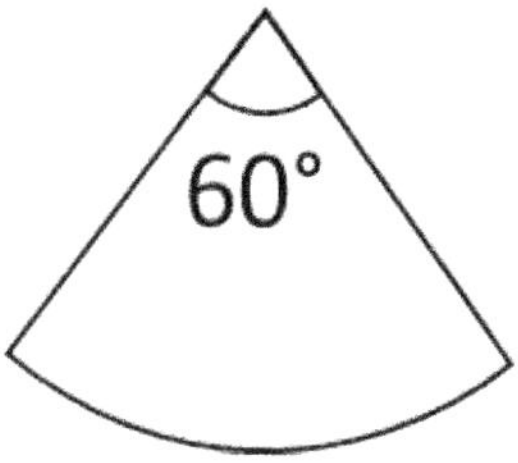

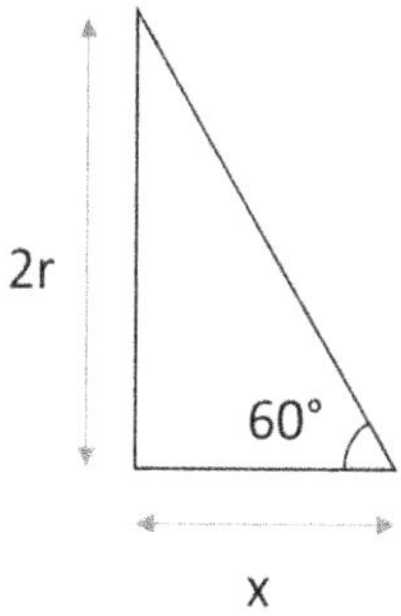

Question 177: B

$(2r)^2 = r^2 + x^2$

$3r^2 = x^2$

$x = \sqrt{3}r$

$Total\ height = 2r + x = (2 + \sqrt{3})r$

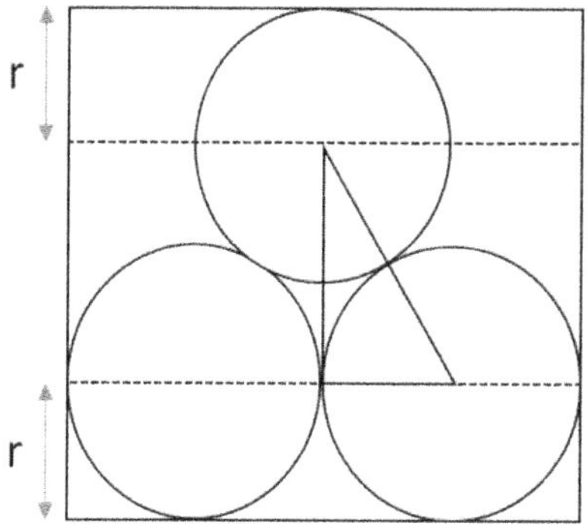

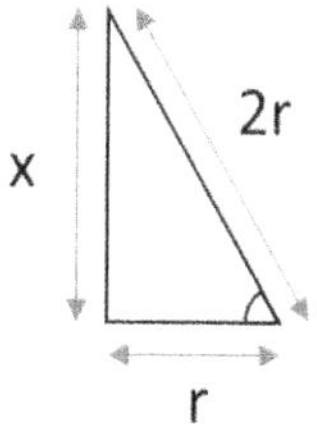

Question 178: A

$V = \frac{1}{3}h \times \text{base area}$

Therefore base area must be equal if h and V are the same

Internal angle = 180° – external ; external = 360°/6 = 60° giving internal angle 120°

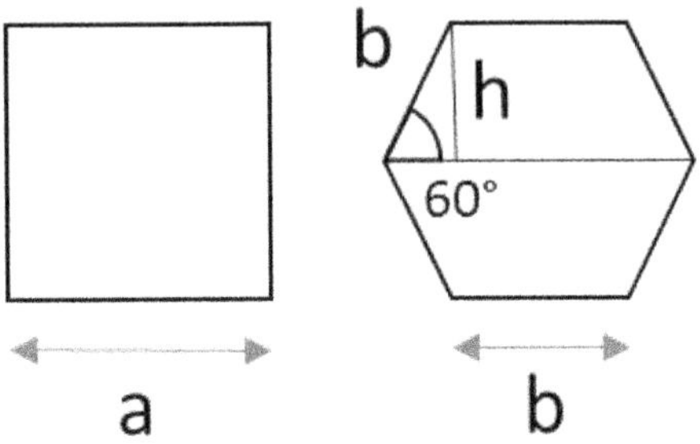

Hexagon is two trapezia of height h where: $\frac{b}{\sin 90°} = \frac{h}{\sin 60°}$

$h = \frac{\sqrt{3}}{2}b$

Trapezium area $= \frac{(2b+b)}{2}\frac{\sqrt{3}}{2}b = \frac{3\sqrt{3}}{4}b^2$

Total hexagon area $= \frac{3\sqrt{3}}{2}b^2$

So from equal volumes: $a^2 = \frac{3\sqrt{3}}{2}b^2$

Ratio: $\sqrt{\frac{3\sqrt{3}}{2}}$

Question 179: C

A cube has 6 sides so the area of 9 cm cube = 6×9^2

9 cm cube splits into 3 cm cubes.

Area of 3 cm cubes = $3^3 \times 6 \times 3^2$

$\frac{6\times3^2\times3^3}{6\times3^2\times3^2} = 3$

Question 180: E

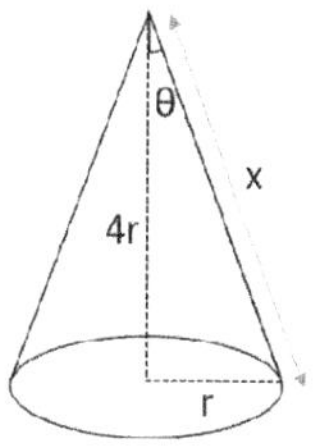

$x^2 = (4r)^2 + r^2$

$x = \sqrt{17}r$

$\frac{\sqrt{17}r}{\sin 90^\circ} = \frac{r}{\sin\theta}$

$\theta = \sin^{-1}\left(\frac{1}{\sqrt{17}}\right)$

Question 181: C

0 to 200 is 180 degrees so: $\frac{\theta}{180} = \frac{70}{200}$

$\theta = \frac{7\times180}{20} = 63^\circ$

Question 182: C

Since the rhombi are similar, the ratio of angles = 1

Length scales with square root of area so length B = $\sqrt{10}$ length A

$$\frac{angle\ A/angle\ B}{length\ A/length\ B} = \frac{1}{\sqrt{10}/1} = \frac{1}{\sqrt{10}}$$

Question 183: E

$y = \ln(2x^2)$

$e^y = 2x^2$

$x = \sqrt{\frac{e^y}{2}}$

As the input is -x, the inverse function must be $f(x) = -\sqrt{\frac{e^y}{2}}$

Question 184: C

$log_8(x)$ and $log_{10}(x) < 0$; $x^2 < 1$; $\sin(x) \le 1$ and $1 < e^x < 2.72$

So e^x is largest over this range

Question 185: C

$x \propto \sqrt{z}^3$

$\sqrt{2}^3 = 2\sqrt{2}$

Question 186: A

The area of the shaded part, that is the difference between the area of the larger and smaller circles, is three times the area of the smaller so: $\pi r^2 - \pi x^2 = 3\pi x^2$. From this, we can see that the area of the larger circle, radius x, must be 4x the smaller one so: $4\pi r^2 = \pi x^2$

$4r^2 = x^2$

$x = 2r$

The gap is $x - r = 2r - r = r$

Question 187: D

$x^2 + 3x - 4 \geq 0$

$(x-1)(x+4) \geq 0$

Hence, $x - 1 \geq 0$ or $x + 4 \geq 0$

So $x \geq 1$ or $x \geq -4$

Question 188: C

$\frac{4}{3}\pi r^3 = \pi r^2$

$\frac{4}{3}r = 1$

$r = \frac{3}{4}$

Question 189: B

When $x^2 = \frac{1}{x}$; $x = 1$

When $x > 1, x^2 > 1, \frac{1}{x} < 1$

When $x < 1, x^2 < 1, \frac{1}{x} > 1$

Range for $\frac{1}{x}$ is $x > 0$

Non-inclusive so: $0 < x < 1$

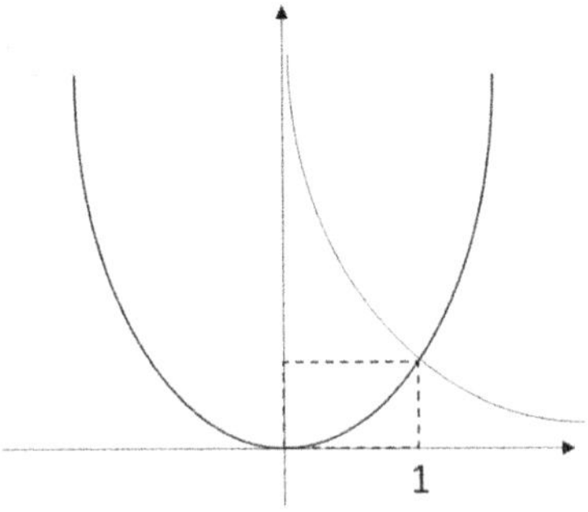

Question 190: A

Don't be afraid of how difficult this initially looks. If you follow the pattern, you get (e-e) which = 0. Anything multiplied by 0 gives zero.

Question 191: C

For two vectors to be perpendicular their scalar product must be equal to 0.

Hence, $\begin{pmatrix}-1\\6\end{pmatrix}\cdot\begin{pmatrix}2\\k\end{pmatrix}=0$

$\therefore\ -2+6k=0$

$k=\frac{1}{3}$

Question 192: C

The point, q, in the plane meets the perpendicular line from the plane to the point p.

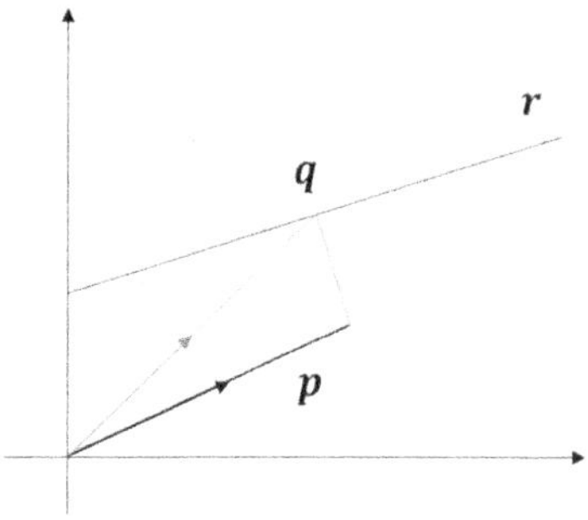

$\boldsymbol{q}=-3\boldsymbol{i}+\boldsymbol{j}+\lambda_1(\boldsymbol{i}+2\boldsymbol{j})$

$\overrightarrow{PQ}=-3\boldsymbol{i}+\boldsymbol{j}+\lambda_1(\boldsymbol{i}+2\boldsymbol{j})+4\boldsymbol{i}+5\boldsymbol{j}$

$=\begin{pmatrix}-7+\lambda_1\\-4+2\lambda_1\end{pmatrix}$

PQ is perpendicular to the plane $\boldsymbol{r}$ therefore the dot product of $\overrightarrow{PQ}$ and a vector within the plane must be 0.

$\begin{pmatrix}-7+\lambda_1\\-4+2\lambda_1\end{pmatrix}\cdot\begin{pmatrix}1\\2\end{pmatrix}=0$

$\therefore\ -7+\lambda_1-8+4+\lambda_1=0$

$\lambda_1=3$

$\overrightarrow{PQ}=\begin{pmatrix}-4\\2\end{pmatrix}$

The perpendicular distance from the plane to point p is therefore the modulus of the vector joining the two $\overrightarrow{PQ}$:

$|\overrightarrow{PQ}|=\sqrt{(-4)^2+2^2}=\sqrt{20}=2\sqrt{5}$

Question 193: E

$-1 + 3\mu = -7\ ;\ \mu = -2$

$2 + 4\lambda + 2\mu = 2\ \therefore\ \lambda = 1$

$3 + \lambda + \mu = k\ \therefore\ k = 2$

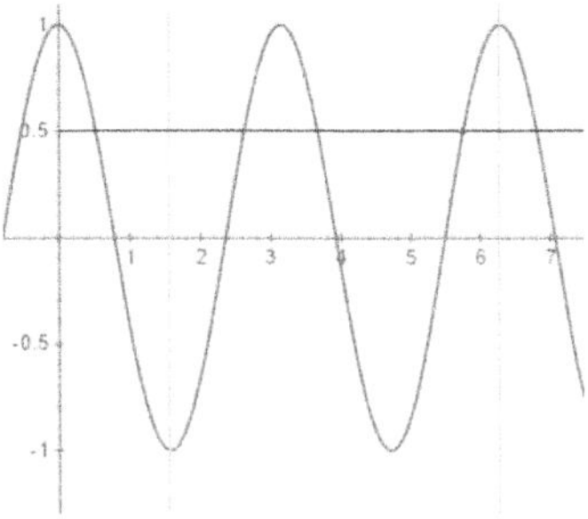

Question 194: E

$\sin\left(\frac{\pi}{2} - 2\theta\right) = \cos(2\theta)$

Root solution to $\cos(\theta) = 0.5$

$\theta = \frac{\pi}{3}$

Solution to $\cos(2\theta) = 0.5$

$\theta = \frac{\pi}{6}$

Largest solution within range is: $2\pi - \frac{\pi}{6} = \frac{(12-1)\pi}{6} = \frac{11\pi}{6}$

Question 195: A

$\cos^4(x) - \sin^4(x) \equiv \{\cos^2(x) - \sin^2(x)\}\{\cos^2(x) + \sin^2(x)\}$

From difference of two squares, then using Pythagorean identity $\cos^2(x) + \sin^2(x) = 1$

$\cos^4(x) - \sin^4(x) \equiv \cos^2(x) - \sin^2(x)$

But double angle formula says: $\cos(A + B) = \cos(A)\cos(B) - \sin(A)\sin(B)$

$\therefore if\ A = B, \cos(2A) = \cos(A)\cos(A) - \sin(A)\sin(A)$

$= \cos^2(A) - \sin^2(A)$

So, $\cos^4(x) - \sin^4(x) \equiv \cos(2x)$

Question 196: C

Factorise: $(x + 1)(x + 2)(2x - 1)(x^2 + 2) = 0$

Three real roots at $x = -1, x = -2, x = 0.5$ and two imaginary roots at 2i and -2i

Question 197: C

An arithmetic sequence has constant difference d so the sum increases by d more each time:

$u_n = u_1 + (n-1)d$

$\sum_1^n u_n = \frac{n}{2}\{2u_1 + (n-1)d\}$

$$\sum_1^8 u_n = \frac{8}{2}\{4 + (8-1)3\} = 100$$

Question 198: E

$\binom{n}{k} 2^{n-k}(-x)^k = \binom{5}{2} 2^{5-2}(-x)^2$

$= 10 \times 2^3 x^2 = 80x^2$

Question 199: A

Having already thrown a 6 is irrelevant. A fair die has equal probability $P = \frac{1}{6}$ for every throw.

For three throws: $P(6 \cap 6 \cap 6) = \left(\frac{1}{6}\right)^3 = \frac{1}{216}$

Question 200: D

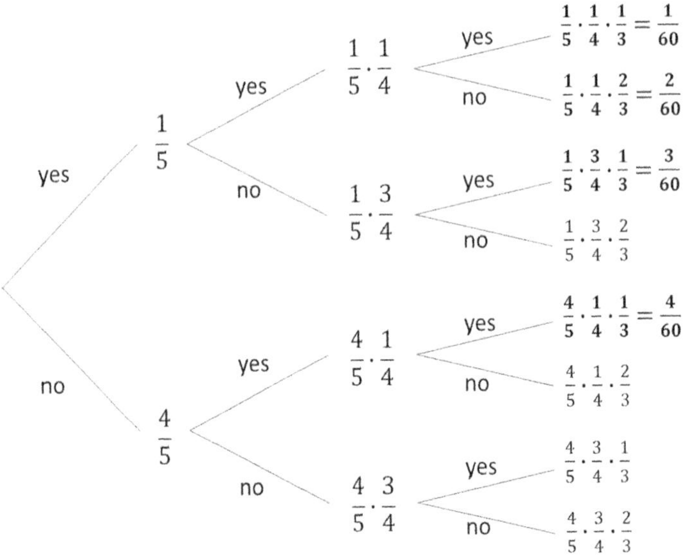

Total probability is sum of all probabilities:

$= P(Y \cap Y \cap Y) + P(Y \cap Y \cap N) + P(Y \cap N \cap Y) + P(N \cap Y \cap Y)$

$= \frac{1}{60} + \frac{2}{60} + \frac{3}{60} + \frac{4}{60} = \frac{10}{60} = \frac{1}{6}$

Question 201: C

$P[(A \cup B)'] = 1 - P[(A \cup B)]$

$= 1 - \{P(A) + P(B) - P(A \cap B)\}$

$= 1 - \frac{2+6-1}{8} = \frac{3}{8}$

Question 202: D

Using the product rule: $\frac{dy}{dx} = x \cdot 4(x+3)^3 + 1 \cdot (x+3)^4$

$= 4x(x+3)^3 + (x+3)(x+3)^3$

$= (5x+3)(x+3)^3$

Question 203: A

$\int_1^2 \frac{2}{x^2} dx = \int_1^2 2x^{-2}\, dx =$

$\left[\frac{2x^{-1}}{-1}\right]_1^2 = \left[\frac{-2}{x}\right]_1^2$

$= \frac{-2}{2} - \frac{-2}{1} = -1$

Question 204: D

Express $\frac{5i}{1+2i}$ in the form $a + bi$

$\frac{5i}{1+2i} \cdot \frac{1-2i}{1-2i}$

$= \frac{5i+10}{1+4} - \frac{5i+10}{5}$

$= i + 2$

Question 205: B

$7\log_a(2) - 3\log_a(12) + 5\log_a(3)$

$7\log_a(2) = \log_a(2^7) = \log_a(128)$

$3\log_a(12) = \log_a(1728)$

$5\log_a(3) = \log_a(243)$

This gives: $\log_a(128) - \log_a(1728) + \log_a(243)$

$= \log_a\left(\frac{128\times243}{1728}\right) = \log_a(18)$

Question 206: E

Functions of the form quadratic over quadratic have a horizontal asymptote. Divide each term by the highest order in the polynomial i.e. x^2:

$$\frac{2x^2 - x + 3}{x^2 + x - 2} = \frac{2 - \frac{1}{x} + \frac{3}{x^2}}{1 + \frac{1}{x} - \frac{2}{x^2}}$$

$$\lim_{x\to\infty}\left(\frac{2 - \frac{1}{x} + \frac{3}{x^2}}{1 + \frac{1}{x} - \frac{2}{x^2}}\right) = \frac{2}{1} \quad i.e.\, y \to 2$$

$x^2 + x - 2 = 4x^2 - 2x + 6$

$3x^2 - 3x + 8 = 0$

$3 \pm \sqrt{9}$

So, the asymptote is $y = 2$

Question 207: A

$1 - 3e^{-x} = e^x - 3$

$4 = e^x + 3e^{-x} = \frac{(e^x)^2}{e^x} + \frac{3}{e^x} = \frac{(e^x)^2+3}{e^x}$

This is a quadratic equation in (e^x): $(e^x)^2 - 4(e^x) + 3 = 0$

$(e^x - 3)(e^x - 1) = 0$

So $e^x = 3, x = \ln(3)$ or $e^x = 1, x = 0$

Question 208: D

Rearrange into the format: $(x + a)^2 + (y + b)^2 = r^2$

$(x - 3)^2 + (y + 4)^2 - 25 = 12$

$(x - 3)^2 + (y + 4)^2 = 47$

$\therefore r = \sqrt{47}$

Question 209: C

$\sin(-x) = -\sin(x)$

$\int_0^a 2\sin(-x)\,dx = -2\int_0^a \sin(x)\,dx = -2[\cos(x)]_0^a = \cos(a) - 1$

Solve $\cos(a) - 1 = 0 \ \therefore a = 2k\pi$

Or simply the integral of any whole period of sin(x) = 0 i.e. $a = 2k\pi$

Question 210: E

$\frac{2x+3}{(x-2)(x-3)^2} = \frac{A}{(x-2)} + \frac{B}{(x-3)} + \frac{C}{(x-3)^2}$

$2x + 3 = A(x - 3)^2 + B(x - 2)(x - 3) + C(x - 2)$

When $x = 3, (x - 3) = 0$, $C = 9$

When $x = 2$, $(x - 2) = 0$, $A = 7$

$2x + 3 = 7(x - 3)^2 + B(x - 2)(x - 3) + 9(x - 2)$

For completeness: Equating coefficients of x^2on either side: $0 = 7 + B$ which gives: $B = -7$

Section 2 Worked Solutions

Q	A	Q	A	Q	A	Q	A	Q	A
1.1	C	**3.1**	B	**5.1**	C	**7.1**	E	**9.1**	C
1.2	D	**3.2**	E	**5.2**	B	**7.2**	D	**9.2**	B
1.3	C	**3.3**	B	**5.3**	A	**7.3**	B	**9.3**	A
1.4	C	**3.4**	D	**5.4**	C	**7.4**	D	**9.4**	C
2.1	A	**4.1**	B	**6.1**	E	**8.1**	C	**10.1**	C
2.2	E	**4.2**	D	**6.2**	A	**8.2**	D	**10.2**	E
2.3	D	**4.3**	C	**6.3**	B	**8.3**	A	**10.3**	D
2.4	A	**4.4**	A	**6.4**	A	**8.4**	D	**10.4**	A

Question 1.1: C

The distance the ball travels is maximised when the angle to the horizontal at which the golfer hits the ball is 45°.

Question 1.2: D

The velocity at which the golfer hits the ball is $\frac{2\pi L}{T}$ = 62.5m/s.

Question 1.3: C

Vertical velocity is $vsin(45)$, acceleration is downwards $g = -10$

The time t the ball spends in the air is twice the time to reach peak height when v= 0. Assuming that the initial velocity of the ball is approximately v= 60 we could calculate:

$\Delta v = at;\ t = 2v\frac{sin(45°)}{g} = 6\sqrt{2}$

Question 1.4: C

Time spent for vertical motion is the same as that for horizontal. Assuming air resistance is negligible. The distance D the ball travels in that time is then $D = v\_h\, t = vcos(45°)t = 360\ m$.

Question 2.1: A

The mass of the Moon is $M_{Moon}=\rho_{Moon}$ x $V_{Moon}=\rho_{Moon}$ x $4r_{Moon}^3$ x $\pi/3$

As density and radius are different, substitute in for $(\frac{3}{4})\ \rho$ and $(\frac{1}{4})r$ to make it in terms of the earth's data: $M_{Moon} = \frac{3}{4}\ \rho_{(earth)}\ x\ \frac{4}{3}\ \ x\ \left(\frac{r_{earth}}{4}\right)^3\ \ x\ \pi = \frac{\rho_{earth}\ x\ r_{earth}^3\ x\ \pi}{64}$

Question 2.2: E

The gravitational force is $F = G\frac{Mm}{R^2}$. According to Newton's second law $F = ma$

Therefore, the gravitational acceleration is $= \frac{GM}{R^2}$. Using concepts applied in question 2.1 one can write $M = \rho.V = \frac{4}{3}\rho\pi R^3$. Applied the equation for the mass of the earth into the equation for the gravitational acceleration one would have $g_{Earth}= G\rho\frac{4}{3}\pi R$

Question 2.3: D

Repeating the same calculations done in the Question 2.2 but this time for the moon, one would have

$g_{moon} = \frac{GM_{moon}}{R^2}$. Expressing the acceleration of the moon in terms of the density and radius of the earth (as in Question 2.1), one could write: $g_{moon} = \frac{G*\rho_{earth}*R_{earth}^3*\pi}{\frac{R_{earth}^2}{16}} = 16G\rho_{earth}R_{earth}\pi$

Taking the ration of the two (using the answer form question 2.2) and simplify gives $g_{moon}= (3/16)g_{earth}$

Question 2.4: A

$F = mg = \frac{mv^2}{r}$ for a satellite. So, v is proportional to the square root of g therefore the speed will decrease with decreased g by a factor of $\sqrt{(\frac{3}{16})}$.

Question 3.1: B

$$\frac{1}{Rtotal} = \frac{1}{R} + \frac{1}{R} \ therefore\ Rtotal = \frac{R}{2}$$

Question 3.2: E

Evaluate each group in parallel as one component and then add in series to first:

$$\boldsymbol{R\_total = R + 1/(1/(R + 1/(\tfrac{1}{R} + \tfrac{1}{R})) + 1/(R + 1/(\tfrac{1}{R} + \tfrac{1}{R}))}$$

$$\boldsymbol{= R + 1/(2/(R + \tfrac{R}{2})) = R + 1/(2/(\tfrac{3R}{2})) = R + \frac{3R}{4} = \frac{7R}{4}}$$

Question 3.3: B

Using the equation for the voltage in the circuit $V=IR_{total}$, one can use total resistance from previous question.

Expressing it in terms of R: $V = I\frac{7}{4}R => R = \frac{4}{7}\frac{V}{I}$

$$R = \frac{4}{7} * \frac{1.4}{2} = 0.4\ \Omega$$

Question 3.4: D

Using the equation for the power in terms of voltage and current P=VI, one can use the total current and voltage from question 3.1.

$P = 1.4x\ 2 = 2.8\ W$

Question 4.1: B

Since the position is given by the equation $x = 10 + 1.5t^3$, and knowing that the velocity is a rate of change of the position, that is $v = \frac{dx}{dt}$, we have:

$$v = \frac{dx}{dt} = \frac{d(10+1.5t^3)}{dt} = 4.5t^2$$

Question 4.2 D

The acceleration represents the rate of change of the velocity, so if one takes the derivative of the velocity in relation to time, one will have expression for acceleration.

$a = \frac{dv}{dt} = \frac{d(4.5t^2)}{dt} = 9.0t$ Equaling the acceleration to zero $a = 9.0t^2 = 0 => t = 0$

Question 4.3 C

One can apply the equation for the position of the particle to figure out the total displacement of the particle for the given interval.

$t = 2s => x_1 = 22\ m$ $\qquad$ $t = 10s => x_2 = 1510\ m$

Total displacement: $\Delta x = x_2 - x_1 = 1488\ \ m$

Average velocity: $\Delta v = \frac{\Delta x}{\Delta t} = \frac{1488}{8} = 186\ m/s$

Question 4.4 A

First step is to calculate the average velocity of the ball for the first 5 seconds.

$t = 5s => x = 197.5\ m$ which is equal to the total displacement

Average velocity: $\Delta v = \frac{\Delta x}{\Delta t} = \frac{197.5}{5} = 39.5$

Considering that an elastic collision is in place, the total energy transferred to the wall is equal to Kindest energy of the ball in the moment of collision. Thus: $E = \frac{mv^2}{2} = \frac{(m*39.5^2)}{2} \approx 780m\ J$

Question 5.1: C
Gravitational potential energy = mgh
= $(700 + 800)\ x\ 10\ x\ 7\ = 105{,}000\ J$

Question 5.2: B
Power = Energy / Time = 3500 W
Assuming 100% efficiency, energy put in is gravitational potential from previous

Question 5.3: A
Average velocity = Distance / Time=0.23 ms^{-1}

$$Kinetic\ energy\ = \frac{mv^2}{2} = 40.8\ J$$

Question 5.4: C
The lift accelerates with the acceleration *a* for t=10 s, then it uniformly moves for t=10 s with the speed *v=at* and then it decelerates with the same acceleration for t=10s.

$$h\ = \frac{at^2}{2}\ +\ vt\ + \frac{at^2}{2}\ =\ 2at^2\ =\ 2vt$$

$$v\ =\ \frac{h}{2t} = 0.35\ ms^{-1}$$

Question 6.1: E
One can apply Newton's second law to block 2 and solve the question. $F_2 = m_2a_2$

The component of the weight pulling the block down can be expressed as: $F_{x2} = m_2gsin\alpha$

The component of the weight in the y direct (equals to the normal reaction against the ramp) can be expressed as: $F_{y2} = m_2g\ cos\alpha$. Therefore, the friction force can be expressed as: $F_{f1-2} = F_{y2}\mu_2 = m_2gcos\alpha\mu_2$

Finally, applying Newton's second law the acceleration of block 2 can be expressed:

$m_2a_2 = m_2g\ sin\alpha - \mu_2m_2g\ cos\alpha \Rightarrow a_2 = g\ (sin\alpha - \mu_2cos\alpha)$

Question 6.2: A
Same reasoning applied in question 6.1 can be applied to block 1 to express the acceleration of block.

The component of the weight pulling the block down can be expressed as:
$F_{x1} = m_1 g sin\alpha$

The component of the weight in the y direct (equals to the normal reaction against the ramp) can be expressed as: $F_{y1} = m_1 g\ cos\alpha$. Therefore, the friction force can be expressed as: $F_{f1-2} = F_{y1}\mu_1 = m_1 g cos\alpha \mu_1$

Applying Newton's second law: $m_1 a_1 = m_1 g\ sin\alpha - \mu_1 m_1 g\ cos\alpha \Rightarrow a_1 = g\ (sin\alpha - \mu_1 cos\alpha)$

Question 6.3: B
To determine the acceleration of m_1 in respect to m_2, one can simply subtract the acceleration of block 1 in respect to the plane and the acceleration of block in respect to the plane to derive the acceleration of block 1 in respect to block 2:

$a_1' = a_1 - a_2 = g\ (sin\alpha - \mu_1 cos\alpha) - g\ (sin\alpha - \mu_2 cos\alpha) = g\ cos\alpha\ (\mu_2 - \mu_1)$

Question 6.4: A
When forces balance $m_2 g\ sin\alpha = \mu_2 m_2 g\ cos\alpha$ so $\mu_2 = sin\alpha / cos\alpha = tan\alpha$

Question 7.1 E
This question can be easily solved if the total time is divided in small intervals of time and analyzed individually. 30 min corresponds to 1800s. According to the graph:
Interval: 0 – 100 s

Accelerated movement: $a = \frac{\Delta v}{\Delta t} = \frac{20}{100} = 0.2\ m/s^2$

Distance can be then calculated: $v^2 = v_o{}^2 + 2ad \Rightarrow d_{0-100} = \frac{v^2 - v_o{}^2}{2a} = \frac{20^2 - 0}{2*0.2} = 1000\ m$

For Interval: 100 – 800 s:
Constant velocity: $v = 20\frac{m}{s} => d_{100-800} = v * \Delta t = 20 * 700 = 1400\ m$

For Interval 800 – 1000 s:
Decelerated movement: $a = \frac{\Delta v}{\Delta t} = -\frac{20}{200} = -0.1\frac{m}{s^2}$
Distance can be calculated: $v^2 = v_o{}^2 + 2ad => d_{800-1000} = \frac{v^2 - v_o{}^2}{2a} = \frac{0-20^2}{2*-0.1} = 2000\ m$

For Interval 1000 – 1600 s:
The velocity is zero which means that the car is not moving.

For Interval 1600 – 1800 s:
Accelerated movement: $a = \frac{\Delta v}{at} = \frac{15}{200} = 0.075\ m/s^2$

Distance can be calculated: $v^2 = v_o{}^2 + 2ad => d_{1600-1800} = \frac{15^2-0}{2*0.075} = 1500\ m$

Total Distance: $D = 1000 + 1400 + 2000 + 1500 = 5900\ m$

Question 7.2: D
Using information from previous question one can write the expression for the velocity in the interval 1600 – 1800 s. $v = v_o + at = 0 + 0.075t$

No calculation is needed for this problem if the student realizes that the integration of the velocity for that in the interval will give you the distanced travelled by the car in the interval, which has already been computed in the previous question and it 1500 m.

The integration then will be:

$$\int_{1600}^{1800} v\, dt = \int_0^{200} 0.075\, t\, dt = 0.0375t^2{}_0^{200} = 0.0375(200^2)$$
$$= 1500m$$

Question 7.3: B

At t= 900s the car is subjected to an acceleration of $|a| = 0.1m/s^2$
According to Newton's second law $F = ma => 1000 * 0.1 = 100N$

Question 7.4: A

At t= 50s the car is subjected to an acceleration of $|a| = 0.2m/s^2$, leading to an applied force of $F = ma = 1000 * 0.2 = 200\ N$

The force applied to the car by the engine is constant throughout the whole interval. Then one can calculate the average work done by the engine: $W = Fd = 200 * 1000 = 200000\ J$

Finally, one can calculate the power: $P = \frac{W}{\Delta t} = \frac{200000}{100} = 2000W$

Question 8.1: C

One can observe that the force applied to the particle is positive up to x = 3 m, which means that the particle is being accelerated up to that point, and its velocity is increasing. After x = 3 m, the force applied to the particle starts to be negative, which means that the particle is being decelerated and its velocity decreasing after x = 3m. Therefore, the velocity and consequently the kinetic energy is maximum at x = 3 m.

Question 8.2: D

Following similar reasoning as in the previous question, and knowing the maximum velocity happens at x= 3m, consequently, one can affirm the kinetic energy is maximum at x = 3 m.

Question 8.3: A

One can get this answer by analyzing the graph. The area under the curve of a graph Force x distance will give the work that has been done to the particle. Since the particle is at rest at x = 0, its kinetic energy and velocity are zero at x = 0. The area from x = 0 to 3, represents the work done to the particle by the positive force and the area from x= 3 to 6, represents the work done to the particle by the negative force; that is, the force in the opposite direction of the positive force. Since the two areas cancel each other, at x=6 all the work that has previous been done the particle by the positive force will have been cancelled by the work done by the negative force (acting in the opposite direction). Therefore, the kinetic energy of the particle at x=0 is zero and, consequently, its velocity is also zero.

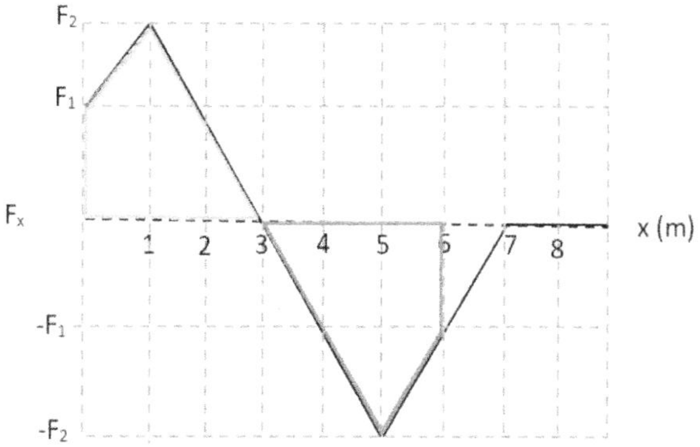

Question 8.4: D

After x=6m the force is acting in the opposite direction compared to what it was before at x=2m. Therefore, the acceleration vector is also pointing the opposite direction as it was in x=2m.

Question 9.1: C

This set of questions involves knowledge of accelerated and decelerated movement and conservation of energy. When the ball is throw up in the air, it is subjected to the gravitational acceleration, pointing downwards to the centre of Earth. Therefore, the acceleration is constant and negative, with the velocity reaching zero at the highest point and the same velocity, in modulus, when it returns to the starting point. Option C is the only one that represents such behaviour.

Question 9.2: B

To solve this question, one should consider the conservation of energy, since the resistance of air can be neglected.

Considering the position from which the ball leaves as $h = 0$, the potential energy of the ball will be zero. Since the ball leaves the girl's hand at $v = 15m/s$, its Kinect energy can be calculated:

$$E_k = \frac{1}{2}m.v^2 = \frac{1}{2} * 0.5 * 15^2 = 56.25\,J$$

Considering conservation of energy and knowing that, at the highest position, the kinetic energy of the ball is zero, one can assume that the kinetic energy the ball had at the beginning of its trajectory will be entirely converted in potential energy. From this assumption, one can calculate the high reached by the ball:

$$E_k = E_p => 56.25 = mgh => h = 11.47\ m$$

Question 9.3: A

One can assume this represents a case of decelerated movement with $a = -9.8\ m/s^2$ and easily calculate the time that takes for the ball's velocity be reduced from 15 m/s to 0

$$v = v_o + a.t => t = \frac{(v - v_o)}{a} = \frac{(0 - 15)}{-9.8} = 1.53\ s$$

Question 9.4: C

First, on can calculate the potential energy of the ball 5.0m from the ground:

$$E_{P(5.0m)} = mgh = 0.5 * 9.8 * 5 = 24.5\ J$$

Since, there is conservation of energy, one can subtract the potential energy at 5.0m from the kinetic energy of the ball at the starting point (calculated in question 9.1)

$$E_{k(5.0m)} = 56.25 - 24.5 = 31.75\ J$$

Question 10.1: C

Option C displays the correct representation of the forces with the weight of object 2 pointing downwards towards the centre of Earth, the normal reaction against the surface of the ramp and friction force pointing downwards along the surface of the ramp as a reaction against the eminent movement of object 2 upwards along surface of the ramp.

Question 10.2: E

Considering the object 2 stays at rest in relation to the ramp, one can write:

$$F_f sin\theta + mg = Ncos\theta$$

$$mg = Ncos\theta - F_f sin\theta = Ncos\theta - N\mu sin\theta = N(cos\theta - \mu sin\theta)$$

Question 10.3: D

Following similar reasoning as in previous question, one can write: $Nsin\theta + F_f cos\theta = m_2 a$

$$m_2 a = Nsin\theta + N\mu cos\theta = N(sin\theta + \mu cos\theta)$$

$$a = \frac{N}{m_2}(sin\theta + \mu cos\theta)$$

Question 10.4: A

According to Newton's second law:

$$F = ma = (m_1 + m_2)a => F = 20a => a = \frac{F}{20}$$

Dividing answers for question 10.3 and 10.2 one can get:

$$\frac{a}{g} = \frac{(sin\theta + \mu cos\theta)}{cos\theta - \mu sin\theta}$$

$$\frac{F}{20g} = \frac{(sin\theta + \mu cos\theta)}{cos\theta - \mu sin\theta} => F = 20g * \frac{(sin\theta + \mu cos\theta)}{cos\theta - \mu sin\theta} = 219N$$

Final Advice

Arrive well rested, well fed and well hydrated

The ENGAA is an intensive test, so make sure you're ready for it. Ensure you get a good night's sleep before the exam (there is little point cramming) and don't miss breakfast. If you're taking water into the exam then make sure you've been to the toilet before so you don't have to leave during the exam. Make sure you're well rested and fed in order to be at your best!

Move on

If you're struggling, move on. In the time it takes to answer one hard question, you could gain three times the marks by answering the easier ones. Be smart to score points- especially in section 2 where some questions are far easier than others and different questions are worth different marks.

Afterword

Remember that the route to a high score is your approach and practice. Don't fall into the trap that "*you can't prepare for the ENGAA*"– this could not be further from the truth. With knowledge of the test, some useful time-saving techniques and plenty of practice, you can dramatically boost your score.

Work hard, never give up and do yourself justice.

Good luck!

Acknowledgements

I would like to express my sincerest thanks to the many people who helped make this book possible, especially the Oxbridge Tutors who shared their expertise in compiling the huge number of questions and answers.

Rohan

About UniAdmissions

UniAdmissions is an educational consultancy that specialises in supporting **applications to Medical School and to Oxbridge**.

Every year, we work with hundreds of applicants and schools across the UK. From free resources to our *Ultimate Guide Books* and from intensive courses to bespoke individual tuition – with a team of **300 Expert Tutors** and a proven track record, it's easy to see why UniAdmissions is the **UK's number one admissions company**.

To find out more about our support like **ENGAA tuition** check out www.uniadmissions.co.uk/ENGAA

Your Free Book

Thanks for purchasing this Ultimate Guide Book. Readers like you have the power to make or break a book – hopefully you found this one useful and informative. *UniAdmissions* would love to hear about your experiences with this book.

As thanks for your time we'll send you another ebook from our Ultimate Guide series absolutely FREE!

How to Redeem Your Free Ebook

1) Etiher scan the QR code or find the book you have on your Amazon purchase history or your email receipt to help find the book on Amazon.

2) On the product page at the Customer Reviews area, click 'Write a customer review'. Write your review and post it! Copy the review page or take a screen shot of the review you have left.

3) Head over to www.uniadmissions.co.uk/free-book and select your chosen free ebook! You can choose from:

- The Ultimate ENGAA Guide
- ENGAA Mock Papers
- ENGAA Past Paper Worked Solutions
- The Ultimate Oxbridge Interview Guide
- The Ultimate UCAS Personal Statement Guide

Your ebook will then be emailed to you – it's as simple as that!

Alternatively, you can buy all the above titles at **uniadmisions.co.uk/our-books**

ENGAA Online Course

If you're looking to improve your ENGAA score in a short space of time, our **ENGAA Online Course** is perfect for you. The ENGAA Online Course offers all the content of a traditional course in a single easy-to-use online package available instantly after checkout. The online videos are just like the classroom course, ready to eatch and re-watch at home or on-the-go and all with our expert Oxbridge tuition and advice.

You'll get full access to all of our ENGAA resources including:

- ✓ Copy of our acclaimed book "The Ultimate ENGAA Guide"
- ✓ Full access to extensive ENGAA online resources including:
- ✓ 2 complete mock papers
- ✓ 250 practice questions
- ✓ Fully worked solutions for all ENGAA past papers
- ✓ 4 hours online on-demand lecture series
- ✓ Ongoing Tutor Support until Test date – never be alone again.

The course is normally £99 but you can get **£ 20 off** by using the code "*UAONLINE20*" at checkout.

www.uniadmissions.co.uk/engaa-online-course

£20 VOUCHER:
UAONLINE20

Printed in Great
Britain
by Amazon

31080615R00112